WOMEN AT WAR

IN UNIFORM

1939–1945

CAROL

HARRIS

SUTTON PUBLISHING

First published in the United Kingdom in 2003 by
Sutton Publishing Limited · Phoenix Mill
Thrupp · Stroud · Gloucestershire · GL5 2BU

British Library Cataloguing in Publication Data
A catalogue record for this book is available from the British Library.

ISBN 0-7509-2633-3

Typeset in 11/15 pt Ehrhardt MT.
Typesetting and origination by
Sutton Publishing Limited.
Printed and bound in England by
J.H. Haynes & Co. Ltd, Sparkford.

Contents

BEAUTY

answers the call . . .

But . . . a smart W.A.A.F. still keeps that
Schoolgirl Complexion

The best-looking women in uniform are those who take care of their skin. A daily bath with Palmolive is a natural beauty treatment, for its rich, velvety, olive-oil lather soothes and beautifies as it cleanses — keeps you "schoolgirl complexion" all over.

PALMOLIVE

3½d. Including Tax.

Below: *Cartoonist Gilbert Wilkinson comments on the wide range in ages of those volunteering for the auxiliary services.* Left: *Advertisers preferred to concentrate on the young and glamorous image of government propaganda.* (*News Chronicle*)

" Well, bye-bye Mummie—and don't forget my advice ! "

Introduction

Just under half a million women served in Britain's forces in the Second World War. The range of duties the military thought suitable for women was initially very limited. At first, it was considered that only young, single women were needed, for domestic, driving and clerical duties, well away from the front or other areas where they might be under fire. These women were to be in a new and specially created service of support personnel, known as the Auxiliary Territorial Service and organised through the Territorial Army.

During the First World War women had fulfilled limited duties for the same reason – to release men to fight at the front – but, as with female civilians, the numbers required in the second conflict were so much greater that it was only a question of time before the government and the military accepted the inevitable: the shortfall in military personnel was such that only by conscription of the nation's women could there be any hope of meeting the manpower demands of this second war. So it was that almost as soon as war broke out, the numbers of women called up, and the range of their duties, began to extend rapidly.

By the time the war was over, many women in the forces had served abroad, and on the home front many worked under fire on anti-aircraft sites in mixed and all-female batteries, during air raids on the cities and towns of Britain, and at remote airfields and ports.

This short book does not attempt to cover completely the various services into which women were deployed, nor all the jobs they did during the war. It does, however, try to give an idea of what life was like in the auxiliary forces and, in women's own words, to record the responses to new and dangerous times. By far the majority of women served in the Auxiliary Territorial Service, and of those, most were in Anti-Aircraft Command, which is why that aspect of the auxiliary forces is recorded here in greater detail.

Looking back, it is easy to forget how close Britain came to losing the Second World War and how vital the contribution of everyone was to avoiding defeat.

Those who were alive at that time and those of us who, subsequently, have learned about their involvement, know that women's contribution, for political and social reasons, was downplayed in the immediate postwar era. Everyone was clear at the time that women had been only temporarily drafted in to 'do a man's job' – a phrase that was repeatedly used before, during and after the war – and so they were expected to go back to their 'proper' place at its end.

There were few films commemorating their efforts and no statues to their memory. It was perhaps understandable at a time when everyone was concerned to 'get back to normal' that this should be the case. As that period passes from living memory and into history, it is in danger of being forgotten completely.

Women all over the country took on harder physical work than before the war, so shoe manufacturers emphasised comfort rather than fashion.

CHAPTER 1
Preparing for War Again

In Britain, at the start of the First World War in August 1914, the main women's groups to offer assistance to the War Office were the Voluntary Aid Detachments (VADs), who were nursing auxiliaries (support workers), and another group of volunteers, the First Aid Nursing Yeomanry (FANY). Unusually, these two groups survived with the same names through to the start of the Second World War, although women in the navy readopted their service title of Women's Royal Naval Service (WRNS) when they were re-formed in 1938.

The FANY was founded in 1908 by Sergeant Major Baker, who had been wounded while serving with Lord Kitchener in the Sudan during the British expedition ten years earlier. Captain Baker, as he later became, saw that ambulances only ferried casualties away to field hospitals: they could not provide essential, life-saving first aid on the battlefield. What was needed, Captain Baker con-cluded, was a band of nurses, based in the field hospitals, who could ride on horseback to tend the wounded where they lay. He decided that

The Countess of Athlone inspects members of the First Aid Nursing Yeomanry Ambulance Unit before their departure for Finland in ambulances supplied by the Canadian Red Cross. (LNA)

each member of the First Aid Nursing Yeomanry, as the new organisation was known, should be trained in first aid, cavalry movements, signalling and camp work so that they could travel with skirmishing parties.

The Voluntary Aid Detachments (VADs) were formed in 1909 and were run by the British Red Cross Society and St John Ambulance. Their members were male and female, and were not nurses but were trained to supplement many nursing duties. VADs also had links with, among other groups, the FANY. Less than one year after the outbreak of the First World War, there were 200 VADs totalling 57,000 men and women.

Other new organisations offering help in 1914 included the Women's Hospital Corps, Women's Emergency Corps, Women's Volunteer Reserve, Women's Defence Relief Corps, Women's Auxiliary Force, Women's Volunteer Motor Drivers and the Home Service Corps. In some, volunteers wore military style uniforms and were trained in signalling, drilling and shooting.

Regardless of the enthusiasm of their volunteers, these organisations were largely unwelcome by the War Office and their organisers' offers of assistance were generally rejected with ill-disguised contempt at the outbreak of hostilities. But many of the female volunteers were welcomed elsewhere in Europe, especially in Serbia, Greece, Belgium, Russia and France. As a result, the various British organisations and individual women were more widely recognised and decorated for their work abroad than in their home country.

The FANY was embraced by the Belgian government and was soon running a hospital in that country. By the time the British War Office wanted

For nearly three years, girls of the ATS and WAAF have been driving throughout the length and breadth of Britain, doing magnificent work, keeping the lines of communication open.

WOMEN Aged 17½ – 43

5ft. 2ins. OR OVER, PHYSICALLY FIT, WANTED NOW

TO BECOME DRIVERS in the ATS and WAAF

No experience needed — you will be trained.* After your training you will be able to drive almost any type of vehicle and do running repairs. It's a grand, open-air life, and it is vitally important work.

Pay starts at 2/- a day and all found. Wives of Servicemen are granted leave to coincide with their husbands' leave whenever possible. In addition to driving, there are over 100 other types of work open now in the ATS and WAAF. Every woman not doing vital work is

asked to join up *to release men for the offensive.* Go to a Recruiting Centre or Employment Exchange. They will find out whether you can be spared from your present work.

If you were born between January 1918 and July 1922, you may now be considered for the ATS or WAAF, but go to the Employment Exchange in the first instance.

Except that if you are under 19 or over 40, you cannot be accepted for the ATS unless you can already drive.

IF you cannot go to a Recruiting Centre or Employment Exchange at once, send in this coupon.	297 Oxford Street, London, W.1. LT.2.
	Please send me *full information about DRIVING* and being trained as a driver in the
	☐ATS ☐WAAF ☐BOTH Tick which you want
	Mrs.⎱ .... Miss⎰ Cross out " Mrs." or " Miss "
	Address ....
	County .... Date of Birth .... In confidence

Recruitment advertisement for women to volunteer as drivers.

the FANY to work as the (first) female drivers for the British Army, the organisation's members, in their khaki officer-style uniforms and navy greatcoats, were driving cars and ambulances, rather than riding on horseback. By the end of the war, the FANY made up a full unit of the Belgian Army and provided convoys for the French Army. Its members won more than sixteen Military Medals, a Legion d'honneur and a Croix de Guerre, and it was the only service to continue throughout the years between the two world wars.

In 1914, one exception to the War Office's general policy of scornful rejection was the Almeric Paget Military Massage Corps, whose masseuses, the forerunners of our present-day chartered physiotherapists, worked in hospitals throughout the UK and Europe. Women doctors, by contrast, formed the Women's Hospital Corps but it was only after they had proved their value in Paris, running a hospital by arrangement with the French Red Cross, that the corps was asked to organise a hospital attached to the Royal Army Medical Corps.

Another exception was the Women's Legion, founded by Lady Londonderry. Its aim was to provide cooks, as the army was facing a severe shortage. It was formally recognised by the Army Council in February 1916.

By the end of that year, the War Office was concerned about shortages in its fighting forces, which even the introduction of conscription had not managed to alleviate. This was partly due to the nature of the conflict; trench warfare resulted in tremendous casualties. Another major factor was the poor health of many of the conscripts – diseases such as rickets and other poverty related conditions predominated and made huge numbers of conscripts unfit for active service. The War Office investigated the numbers and categories of men serving in France and concluded that 12,000 fit men who could be sent to fight at the front were involved in clerical, domestic and signalling duties. The War Office was still reluctant to bring women into the equation but it was obvious that there were too few fit fighting men to ignore the contribution women could bring if they were drafted into these roles.

So British women were called on to volunteer in order to release men from essential work so they could fight at the front. The idea was to provide a force of women to help maintain the fleet and the army in times of war. Some women had already taken on civilian work, for example on buses and trams, in munitions factories and in clerical roles. From 1917, women served in non-combatant roles with the armed forces, at home and abroad, although the War Office refused to enlist them – it insisted they were civilians.

The Women's Army Auxiliary Corps (WAAC) was formed under the patronage of Queen Mary in 1917 and its first director was Mona Chalmers Watson, the sister of Brigadier-General Sir Auckland Geddes, the director of recruiting at the War Office. Helen Gwynne-Vaughan who, as Dame Helen, became head of the ATS in the Second World War, was made head of the WAAC in France. The first WAAC contingent, comprising fourteen cooks and waitresses for the officers' mess in Abbeville, arrived in France in 1917. Very soon, the range of WAAC trades expanded to include laundresses, clerical workers, storekeepers, telegraphers, telephonists and postal workers, bakers, tailors, printers and gardeners. Those who were experienced linguists were attached to the army's intelligence service.

The corps still had no military status and its members were therefore classified by the military as 'camp followers'. However, it soon became clear that those serving in France had to be employed 'as soldiers' and so were subject to military law and protection. In practice, the more brutal punishments meted out to men were ignored for women. Female miscreants were most likely to be fined for their misdemeanours, although they could, in theory, be strapped across a gun carriage and publicly flogged.

The corps certainly looked military; the basic uniform was khaki. Ranks wore a coat frock and felt hats in pudding-basin shape. Officers wore military style jackets and peaked caps in the design of male army officers.

The official reaction by the British armed forces overseas to their performance was generally positive, in sharp contrast to that at home. In France, WAACs distinguished themselves by working hard and bearing many of the same hardships as army soldiers, including accommodation. They dug trenches when air raids threatened and in May 1918, nine WAACs died and seven were wounded during an air raid at Abbeville. The survivors all earned commendations and three women who helped with rescue work were given the Military Medal. Soldiers and officers sent wreaths and attended the funerals the following day.

But to many, especially at home, the very idea of WAACs abroad brought outraged comments and the women were the butt of music hall and soldiers' jokes. Almost immediately they arrived in France, rumours about WAACs' loose morals began to circulate. At one point, Helen Gwynne-Vaughan remarked caustically that there were more reported pregnancies among WAACs in France than the total number serving in that country. The scandals – mostly imagined and spread in part by enemy agents – began to affect morale and recruitment. One rumour given particular credence was that women who joined the WAAC were needed for army brothels.

At the start of 1918, just as the spring offensive meant that major increases in WAAC personnel were required to replace men sent to the front, the numbers applying to be WAACs had dwindled severely. The press and eminent figures such as the Minister of Labour, G.H. Roberts, and Randall Davidson, the Archbishop of Canterbury, spoke up in favour of the corps.

An all-female Commission of Inquiry was established to investigate every aspect of the life of the corps, which now had nearly 22,500 members, over 5,000 of them in France. The commission reported in March 1918. Its detailed investigations had found that rumours of soaring rates of pregnancy among single WAACs, high incidences of venereal disease, incompetence and wrongdoing were unfounded. Instead, the corps impressed the commission with its good discipline and attitude. The official report concluded, 'The general impression of the corps is that of a healthy, cheerful, self-respecting body of young women.' The WAAC received another boost to its morale a few weeks after publication of the report. In April 1918, Queen Mary, who had frequently demonstrated her support for the corps through official visits, became Commander-in-Chief of the renamed Queen Mary's Army Auxiliary Corps. The propa-ganda counter-offensive turned the tide, and by the time it was disbanded in 1919 a total of 57,000 women had served in the corps.

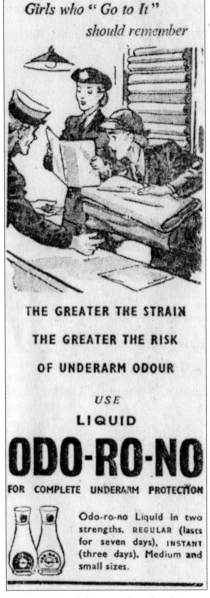

Anyone who did not wash under their armpits for a week probably needed a strong deodorant . . .

Shortly after the WAAC was established, the Royal Navy set up the Women's Royal Naval Service (WRNS) in late 1917, for limited duties on shore previously carried out by ratings in the Royal Navy. Its advertisement in

"*Any complaints ?*"

"*I'm looking forward to my leave, Phoebe, when I can do my spring-cleaning.*"

Women in uniform were a rich source of inspiration to cartoonists such as Gilbert Wilkinson. (*News Chronicle*)

The Times stressed, 'The members of this service will wear a distinctive uniform.' In fact, women in the WRNS wore civilian clothes until January of the following year, when the ankle-length, dressing-gown style overalls in thick, navy serge were, according to costume historian Winifred Ewing, 'a new low for women's uniforms, even then'. Buttoning up the front to a miniature sailor collar, the outfit was worn with heavy boots and the usual pudding-basin-style hat. Officers in the WRNS, by contrast, had a better than average uniform. It was so much better that it changed little when the service was revived at the start of the Second World War. Long skirts were peculiar to the first version but the white shirts, tricorn hat and blue insignia, along with more tailoring than other uniforms, survived into the Second World War and after.

Inevitably, many of the women who served in the WRNS during the First World War did the usual work of cleaning and cooking traditionally associated with women in a domestic environment. But many also worked in wireless telegraphy, and some broke the barrier to WRNS only filling posts on land by working as boats crews. Together with the WAAC, the WRNS also helped form the youngest of the women's forces, the Women's Royal Air Force (WRAF), as a total of 10,000 members from both services were allowed to transfer to this new organisation.

The WRAF was the only service to be formed simultaneously with the men's equivalent. It was created on 1 April 1918, the same day that the Royal Air Force was formed from the Royal Naval Air Service and Royal Flying Corps. The work the WRAF took on was much the same as that of the other women's forces: driving, typing, storekeeping, operating telephone switchboards and orderly duties. As the women proved their worth and came to be regarded as a resource rather than a nuisance, many were trained as fitters and riggers, acetylene welders and electricians.

Uniforms were an even worse problem for the WRAF than for the WRNS. Members transferring from the WRNS and WAAC were told to wear their old uniforms until they wore out, with new WRAF badges attached. Overalls, also

A group of WAACs in the First World War.

with WRAF badges, were issued to some. But the anticipated supplies of uniforms in RAF blue did not arrive and many women had to wear their own clothes for the often dirty work they undertook. When other groups took part in a National Parade of Servicewomen in June 1918, the WRAF could not take part because it had no uniforms.

The war ended or, rather, ground to a halt when Germany ran out of money, in November 1918. Around the time of the armistice, Helen Gwynne-Vaughan, who later became the first director of the Auxiliary Territorial Service, transferred from her post in charge of the WAACs in France to become head of the new WRAF. By the time of its disbandment in 1919, 32,000 women had served in the WRAF. The WRNS and the WRAF were dissolved in 1919. The QMAAC, which had a wider role and was a far larger force than the other two, was not broken up until November 1921.

In peacetime, the First World War and their role in it had an enormous influence on women in Britain, contributing enormously to the social and political upheavals of the interwar years. As civilians, young women continued to outrage others with their behaviour and 'modern manners'. Newspapers and women's magazines regularly criticised women who danced to the new 'degenerate' jazz music, smoked, drank alcohol and applied make-up in public. Shocking also, especially to the older generation, were the slang and swearing of young men and women, made commonplace by, respectively, the arrival of soldiers from the United States in Europe, and their own wartime experiences. Added to this was the growing momentum the First World War gave to the 'Votes for Women' campaign. In 1928, this culminated in women finally being given the vote on the same terms as men – on reaching the age of twenty-one. The changes inevitably highlighted the gap between the generations and older people despaired of the behaviour of young people, in the time-honoured fashion. The general election held that same year was known as the 'Flapper Election', because so many 'flappers', as fashionable young women who flouted convention were termed, were able to vote for the first time.

In the 1930s, these 'Bright Young Things' – another soubriquet popular at the time – became the 'Smart Set', and women especially continued to shock. Social and demographic changes meant that as the 1930s progressed, more and more women were finding employment outside the home. During the First World War, working-class women who might have followed the family tradition of going into domestic service had found that jobs in factories was better paid and often meant shorter hours. As a result, many chose factory work in peacetime, in preference to a life in service and this was a major factor in the decline in the number of servants looking for positions in the already diminishing country houses.

The growth of the suburbs, with their mixture of smaller, middle-class and skilled working-class families, all buying their homes for the first time, was the clearest expression of this enormous social change that had in part been instigated by the war of 1914–18. The trend continued in the Depression years of the 1930s, which encouraged increasing numbers of women to find work, especially when their husbands could not. But it would be a mistake to think that women then had much the same freedoms and attitudes that their contemporaries today might have. Compared to previous generations, their lives were only relatively more liberated. A woman's role, however, was still clearly defined and she had far fewer opportunities to deviate from that path than today, not least because the social upheavals of the Second World War had yet to make their mark.

Anne Varley, who later joined the Auxiliary Territorial Service, commented:

. . . There we were, all boxed in by birth, money, education and prejudice. We lived in a world where girls were brought up in ignorance of sex and advised not to win when competing with boys. And when we grew up, birth control was difficult to come by and rather dirty, abortion was a criminal offence; respectable restaurants refused to serve us in the evening if we were unaccompanied; it was shameful to enter a pub; and no one, not even the police, must ever interfere between a husband and wife, even if she was being beaten. We were the homemakers, the little women and the weaker sex.

As the 1930s progressed, planning for the next, clearly inevitable conflict acquired a growing sense of urgency. The approach was, as usual, to look back to the arrangements from the previous war; plans were drawn up for limited involvement of women in strictly non-combatant roles, far removed from any likely action. Recruitment centred chiefly around calls for women volunteers to help in a wide range of services, civilian and military. Apart from the auxiliary forces supporting the armed equivalents, women were needed for civil defence, the Women's Land Army and in factories, producing munitions, aircraft and other wartime essentials.

In May 1938, seven women, all of whom had played leading roles in organising women's auxiliary forces in the First World War, went to the War Office to discuss the formation of the Women's Territorial Army with Major-General Sir John Brown, deputy director-general of the Territorial Army. At this stage, they all intended that one unified women's organisation, the Auxiliary Territorial Service (ATS), would be created, and its members would be responsible for limited, non-combatant duties. The outcome of those War Office meetings was that the ATS was to be affiliated to Territorial Army units. This meant that although they were called on nationally, the ATS companies were to be raised and run through county territorial and air force units.

Later that year, the Munich Crisis concentrated minds on the likelihood of war. Whatever Neville Chamberlain, the British prime minister, may have said officially about achieving 'peace for our time', the government and the population knew that the piece of paper he waved on his return had at best only bought time in which to prepare for the inevitable.

On 26 September 1938 the War Office published the Conditions of Service leaflet of the Women's Auxiliary Territorial Service. Duties were listed as '(a) Motor driving; (b) Clerical; (c) General duties (cooking, orderlies, store women)'. On 28 September, as Chamberlain prepared to leave for Munich, the *Daily Herald* carried a story in its 'Home Defence' news, headlined, '25,000 women are needed'. With the tempting crosshead, 'May go overseas', it said that the newly formed ATS needed 2,000 officers and 23,000 other ranks. Married or single women were required, between the ages of eighteen and forty-seven for duties at home or overseas and between the ages of forty-seven and fifty-five for local service, near to their homes. Terms of service were that recruits were to serve for four years with an option at the end of that time to re-enlist.

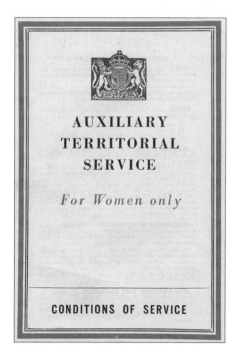

AUXILIARY
TERRITORIAL
SERVICE

For Women only

CONDITIONS OF SERVICE

The Conditions of Service leaflet issued to every member of the ATS. This particular edition was published before the Second World War broke out, when all those in the ATS were volunteers. It ends with the comment that 'Aliens will not be enrolled'. This condition was removed later in the war, enabling refugees, many from Germany and Nazi-occupied Europe, to enlist. (HMSO)

Officers enrolled for an indefinite period. They received a grant of £16 towards the cost of their uniforms. Other ranks were supplied with uniforms free of charge and rations during camping were also to be issued at no cost. Travel to training locations would be paid for and volunteers were told that some other expenses would be paid during training.

The response from women to this call to volunteer was generally better than that from men but even so, by the time war broke out in September 1939, only 17,000 women had enlisted with the auxiliary forces, far short of the 25,000 it was hoped would come forward. Word soon got round that, even so, the government was badly prepared for so many volunteers coming forward in such a short time and uniforms were conspicuous by their absence for many recruits. At this time, too, given prevailing social mores and attitudes to the auxiliary forces in

Candidates for the ATS at an early recruiting drive. These events were held all over the country to bring women into 'the new women's service'. (Kent Messenger Group)

the First World War, it was felt neces-sary repeatedly to address the issue of the reputation that young women had been subject to twenty years before. In 1938, in a *Picture Post* feature encouraging women to volunteer for the auxiliary forces, Mabel Lethbridge wrote, 'In general, the women of the ATS have to live down the bad name given to the WAAC. Dame Helen Gwynne-Vaughan says that the trouble originated as German propaganda. Women of the WAAC were proud of the fact that they were considered important enough for the Germans to take notice of. She adds that less than three per cent of the girls earned the disparagement they got.' Quite how this figure was calculated is not clear.

Either way, officers and instructors were drawn from the ranks of these existing organisations and appointments made on the basis of little more than social or family connections. This was in part a reflection of the way things were done generally in a time when the class system was much more rigid than it is now. It was also typical of the frantic way in which preparations for the war were being made.

Through her connections, notably with her friend Lord Trenchard, first marshal of the RAF, and her cousin the Earl of Munster, who was parliamentary Under-secretary of State for War, Helen Gwynne-Vaughan lobbied successfully

STRENSALL A.T.S. CAMP, 1939
CAMP STANDING ORDERS.
By Miss L. AINSWORTH, Camp Commandant.

NORMAL DAILY ROUTINE.

1.—Reveille	... ...	0700 hrs.
Breakfast	... ...	0800 hrs.
Sick Parade	... ...	0830 hrs.
Dinners	... ...	1230 hrs.
Teas	... ...	1630 hrs.
Supper	... ...	1930 hrs.
Lights out	... ...	2230 hrs.

Buglers of the 1st Bn. K.O.Y.L.I. will sound the above calls. Camp time will be taken from Commandant's Office.

CAMP DUTIES.

2. One of the two Battalions will be detailed daily in Commandant's Orders to find the following duties :—

   (a) Camp Orderly Officer.

   (b) Camp Orderly Serjeant.

   (c) Camp Guards, consisting of 1 Sjt. (or equivalent rank), 1 L/Cpl. (or equivalent rank), 6 volunteers per Battalion. They will mount at 1830 hrs. and dismount at Reveille.

   (d) Camp fire picquet.

   (e) Such working parties as are required.

BOUNDS.

3.—Volunteers may not proceed beyond the Camp bounds without a pass issued by the Group Commanders, unless on duty.

4.—The boundaries of the Camp are marked in red on special Training Maps issued to all groups.

5.—Volunteers are forbidden to enter public houses, Barracks or other Camps, and will be careful to avoid trespassing on private property.

6.—Queen Elizabeth Barracks are out of bounds to all volunteers.

DISCIPLINE.

7.—No noise or talking between lights out and reveille is allowed.

8.—No hawkers other than those authorised are allowed in Camp. Volunteers are forbidden to deal with any other than those authorised.

9.—Motor cars will not be parked in the lines but in the appointed places.

10.—Gratuities to the Regular Soldiers in Camp are forbidden.

11.—Minor breaches of discipline will be dealt with by O.C. Group, under the supervision of Battalion Commanders. Group Commanders will inform Battalion Commanders of the action they take and any serious cases will be reported immediately.

12. **In the event of a fire** the fire piquet will fall in immediately and proceed to the scene of the fire. All tents in the vicinity will immediately be struck by one half of the piquet. The other will form a cordon round the fire for the purpose of keeping off unauthorised spectators. Tents near the scene of the fire will immediately be struck by any volunteers in the vicinity before the arrival of the fire piquet. The Camp Orderly Officer will immediately take charge of arrangements at the scene of the fire. The Guard Commander, 1st Bn. K.O.Y.L.I., Queen Elizabeth Barracks, will be informed as soon as possible.

13.—The greatest care must be taken to avoid setting the grass on fire.

14.—Naked lights are not allowed in tents or shelters, and no lights are to be left burning in an unoccupied tent. No smoking is allowed in the tents.

Y.P.W.—500—6/7/39.

Camp standing orders for Strenshall ATS camp in 1939. The normal routine shows that the day started at 7 a.m. and ended with lights out at 10.30 p.m. In these early days, recruits were usually called volunteers. Order 15 says that 'Volunteers are not allowed to bathe except in the Camp swimming pool at hours to be arranged and notified later.' Under 'Sanitation', volunteers are told, 'Paper will not be thrown about the Camp, but collected and placed in the receptacles provided for the purpose.'

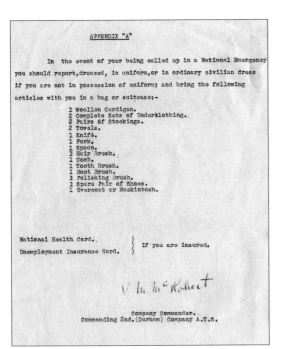

Uniforms were in very short supply just before and at the start of the war.

the First Aid Nursing Yeomanry, the Women's Legion and the Emergency Service, especially, to organise the new service, set up the officer cadre and provide driving instructors. But as the nation found itself on the brink of a war for which it was generally unprepared, the launch of the ATS nonetheless stood out as a master-piece of maladministration.

In the spring of 1939 the WRNS was re-formed, initially on a smaller scale than the 57,000-strong force it had been at the end of the First World War. Only women aged eighteen to fifty and living near naval ports were considered. References from serving

for a woman – herself – to be the first director of the ATS. Her rank, chief controller, was equivalent to that of a major-general in the army and she received a salary equal to two-thirds a major-general's pay. At the same time she promoted the case for a separate women's auxiliary organisation for the RAF, and said that if she were not offered the army post, she would be available to be head of that service instead.

Soon the ATS had officers, other ranks and NCOs (non-commissioned officers). It drew heavily on members of

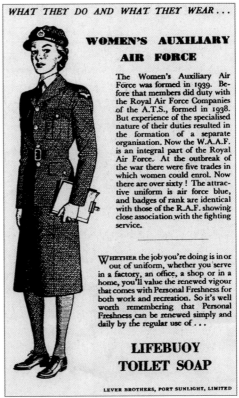

One of a series of advertisements for Lifebuoy soap which featured women in the auxiliary forces.

Women in the Mechanised Transport Corps played an active part right at the start of the war. The corps commandant, Mrs G.M. Cook (left), inspects a WMTC detachment before it leaves for France, early in 1940.

On 2 July 1939, weeks away from the outbreak of war, the ATS, WRNS and WAAF (left to right) were represented at a parade of all the voluntary services held in Hyde Park in London. (The Waverley Book Company) or retired naval men were also necessary, making the service the most selective and nepotistic of the auxiliary forces.

The Women's Auxiliary Air Force was created in July 1939, four months after the WRNS. Its formation was similar to the creation of the WRAF in the First World War; in addition to volunteers from the new recruits to the auxiliary forces, women who were already in the ATS, working alongside the RAF, were drafted into the new service, as well as members of the Women's Legion (Mechanised Transport).

In the eleven months between the Munich Crisis and the declaration of war on 3 September 1939, the various groups marched and trained. Less than two months before war broke out, when the auxiliary services paraded in Hyde Park in July 1939, the event included women from the ATS, WRNS and WAAF. One month later, about half the ATS attended a fortnight-long camp, making themselves familiar with everything from army cooking utensils to sleeping on 'biscuits' (army mattresses made up of three flat sections). As on the civilian home front, however, the numbers and

This 1940 advertisement for Clark's shoes refers to the fact that the authorities were not ready to take on all the women who volunteered at this time, a situation that had changed markedly by 1943.

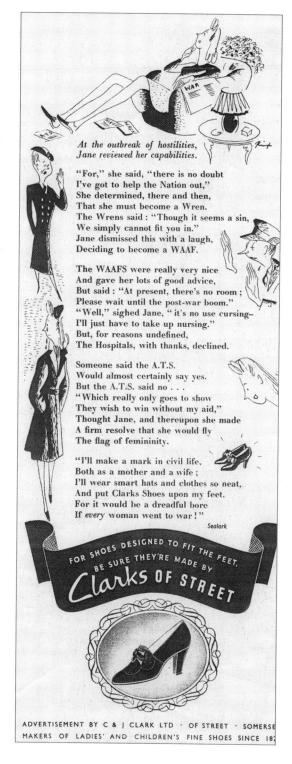

At the outbreak of hostilities, Jane reviewed her capabilities.

"For," she said, "there is no doubt
I've got to help the Nation out,"
She determined, there and then,
That she must become a Wren.
The Wrens said : "Though it seems a sin,
We simply cannot fit you in."
Jane dismissed this with a laugh,
Deciding to become a WAAF.

The WAAFS were really very nice
And gave her lots of good advice,
But said : "At present, there's no room ;
Please wait until the post-war boom."
"Well," sighed Jane, " it's no use cursing-
I'll just have to take up nursing."
But, for reasons undefined,
The Hospitals, with thanks, declined.

Someone said the A.T.S.
Would almost certainly say yes.
But the A.T.S. said no . . .
"Which really only goes to show
They wish to win without my aid,"
Thought Jane, and thereupon she made
A firm resolve that she would fly
The flag of femininity.

"I'll make a mark in civil life,
Both as a mother and a wife ;
I'll wear smart hats and clothes so neat,
And put Clarks Shoes upon my feet.
For it would be a dreadful bore
If *every* woman went to war ! "

Sealark

FOR SHOES DESIGNED TO FIT THE FEET,
BE SURE THEY'RE MADE BY

Clarks OF STREET

ADVERTISEMENT BY C & J CLARK LTD · OF STREET · SOMERSE
MAKERS OF LADIES' AND CHILDREN'S FINE SHOES SINCE 18

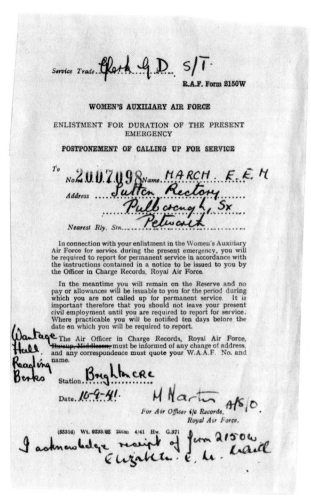

WAAF form for postponement of call-up. At first, many of those who volunteered had to wait until the auxiliary forces could find work, uniforms and billets for them. This was not a problem in the later stages of the war.

range of duties for which women were required expanded rapidly. The overall official intention remained largely the same as twenty years before: women were needed in order to release men to do the fighting; women were not to fire weapons – although, as before, working under enemy fire quickly became an inevitable and regular part of some women's wartime experiences.

When war was declared the three main women's services were still recruiting as fast as they could. By December 1939, 43,000 women and girls had volunteered for the Women's Royal Naval Service, the Women's Auxiliary Air Force and the Auxiliary Territorial Service, most of them in the three months since war had broken out. This far exceeded the target of 25,000 female volunteers, announced just over a year before. The numbers were such that the continuing problems of processing applications and kitting out volunteers were further exacerbated. Many volunteers were frustrated to be told that they had to return home and wait until they were called up.

CHAPTER 2

The Auxiliary Territorial Service

In May 1938, a meeting was held of representatives of three women's services from which support could be drawn for a women's auxiliary force. These were the Emergency Service, the First Aid Nursing Yeomanry and the Women's Legion. All three services were to be combined into one organisation, the Women's Auxiliary Defence Service, to be incorporated into the Territorial Army. Former members of the Emergency Service would provide the training, the Women's Legion would deal with recruitment of trades, such as driving and domestic duties, and the FANY would be responsible for trained personnel and potential officers. After considerable discussion, it was decided that the new force should be called the Auxiliary Territorial Service, not least because the initial letters formed the word ATS, which was preferable to WADS, WAACS or any of the other acronyms which it was felt would encourage ribald comment in the manner of the First World War.

One of the first issues was what to do with the FANY (there was apparently little concern regarding this abbreviation). Since the First World War, the FANYs had been proud of their independence from other, similar organisations of women's forces and frankly had considered themselves to be rather better than the others. The creation of one unifying force seemed logical but in the ATS style and structure, the FANY stood out even more as being different. Unlike the army in general and the ATS in particular, the officers and other ranks of the resolutely volunteer FANY were all equal and informal with each other. They called each other by their surnames and a disproportionate number – including privates – were from army families, so were overly familiar, as far as the ATS was concerned, with male officers. Specifically, army regulations prevented officers from mixing with lower ranks when off duty. The FANY studiously ignored this rule, especially when it came to being seen in public with male relatives who were army officers. Members of the FANY, if not officers already, considered themselves officer material. Even in the narrow, class-defined social order of the 1930s, the FANY

Dame Helen Gwynne-Vaughan,
commandant of the ATS. (The
Waverley Book Company)

were an exclusive, upper-class set of young women, and were often referred to as
the 'mink and manure brigade'. All of them could drive and most could do so
because they were wealthy enough to have their own or family cars.

A major part of the problem was the open hostility between Mary Baxter-Ellis,
commandant of the FANY, and Helen Gwynne-Vaughan. While the new ATS
struggled to organise itself, the FANY recruited 1,500 driver-mechanics and set up
its own training course for officers. Soon conflict arose over officer training for the
new ATS: Helen Gwynne-Vaughan wanted the course, held at the Duke of York's
headquarters in Chelsea, to be compulsory for all would-be ATS officers. Not only
was attendance voluntary, but also members of the FANY MT (motor transport)
were specifically told they did not have to go. This was a clear victory for Mary
Baxter-Ellis over her rival. Other skirmishes were to take place between the
two women and the two services they sought to lead. In these early years, meetings
of the ATS council were often little more than slanging matches between these
women. In the light of this, it was a small wonder that anything was achieved.

The FANYs, under Mary Baxter-Ellis, fought a rearguard action very successfully, deploying their contacts and supporters to counter the efforts of Helen Gwynne-Vaughan and her equally influential friends and relatives. The organisation survived independently as a volunteer force and, as such, kept its own, separate headquarters in London. They also retained their own, smarter khaki uniforms and many wore officer-style Sam Browne belts, which further distinguished them from others in similar uniforms. Despite this, the majority of the FANYs became part of the ATS, and those who joined before 1 September 1941 were able to wear a FANY flash on the shoulder of their uniforms throughout the war. Historically, also, they retained their identity as a distinctive group; the best known – after the war at least – were many of the Free FANYS who had worked undercover in occupied Europe, as members of the Special Operations Executive. Most famous among them were Violette Szabo, whose wartime life and death were portrayed by Virginia McKenna in the 1958 film *Carve Her Name With Pride*, and Odette Churchill, whose work for the resistance, capture and torture by the Gestapo was also the subject of a film, *Odette* (1950).

> Advertisement for the ATS, *Daily Telegraph*, Autumn 1938
>
> Auxiliary Territorial Service (for women). Non-combatant duties with military units. Motor driving, clerical and other services calling for energy and initiative.

The Auxiliary Territorial Service was created in September 1938. Officers and instructors were drawn from the three voluntary organisations which were mainly responsible for setting it up: the First Aid Nursing Yeomanry, the Women's Legion and the Emergency Service. The aim of the ATS was, like the other services, to release men for service at the front and to carry out 'work only women can do'. This meant routine duties, mainly cooking, typing, laundry work and storekeeping.

In his *History of the Second Great War*, an early part-work published weekly during the war, Sir John Hammerton said:

> They take over the cookhouse even with the great old fashioned ovens and cauldrons, and stone steps leading up to it. The ATS take over the cleaning, under the proud name of orderlies; they act the part of kitchen maids and housemaids. Those who have been parlour maids are detailed to wait on officers.

ATS lorry drivers ready for inspection. (Odhams)

The ATS look after the stores, fitting men with boots and their equipment as well as the women. Office routine is so different in the army that a three weeks course of training is given to the clerical company of the ATS at the headquarters of the Eastern Command. They learn, for instance, that in the army a letter is never addressed 'Dear Sir': it is always in memorandum form. They have to become familiar with a variety of forms.

Women motor drivers relieve the men of driving the lighter lorries and transport vans; they drive officers and take messages. In their spare time the drivers attend a course of instruction on maintenance and repairs.

All kinds of women have enrolled: leisured girls, buyers in shops and shop assistants, dressmakers, hairdressers, factory girls and domestic workers, actresses and teachers. They are treated very much as soldiers and it is their pride that it is so. Rations [food] are the same as for men but women have four-fifths of the men's ration; the pay is two-thirds of that of the corresponding army rank. Leave is the same. The freedom of the service is very remarkable and the attitude of the officers is modern and democratic.

*'If only more women would help',
says the soldier in this early
recruiting advertisement – which is a
cheek considering many more women
than men responded to the
government's appeal for volunteers.*

Have you noticed those girls in the A.T.S. uniform,? Smiled a little, admired them perhaps, and thought ' Rather they, than me.' Those girls are helping your menfolk to shorten the war. Cooking and catering for them, transmitting secret messages, working on secret devices. There's a job waiting for you in the A.T.S. . . . a job that you will like. Come and take it quickly.

Write for the full story of the A.T.S. and its opportunities : to The AUXILIARY TERRITORIAL SERVICE. A.G. 18/ n.b.1, Hobart House, Grosvenor Gardens, S.W.1. Or, have a talk at any Employment Exchange, A.T.S. or Army recruiting centre.

30,000 girls are urgently needed in the A.T.S.

*Learning to cook in an emergency
field kitchen.* (Odhams)

ATS in the armoury. One is adjusting a tank rifle, the other cleaning a rifle with a regulation pull-through. (GPU)

The conditions of service, issued in September 1938, allowed members of some companies, whose duties were to be essentially local, to live at home – hardly the 'army way'. Officers enrolled for an indefinite period; other ranks could join up for four years and extend that time by anything between one and four years. The age range was generally eighteen to forty-three years, but ex-servicewomen up to the age of fifty were allowed to rejoin. The minimum height for women was 5 ft 2 in.

Olive Gibbings was among the first to volunteer:

The morning war broke out, we went to the drill hall to see the Territorials arriving for duty. I decided I would join the ATS instead of going in a factory.

I was sent first to Pontefract. Next I went to Camberley on a driving school course – the queen went there some time later. My first posting as a driver was

JOIN THE

ATS

ASK FOR INFORMATION AT THE NEAREST EMPLOYMENT EXCHANGE OR AT ANY ARMY OR ATS. RECRUITING CENTRE

A very elegant image of the ATS, drawn by Abram Games. The idea was to make women in the ATS look as glamorous as possible as the service competed with the WRNS and WAAF for recruits. (Crown Copyright)

with staff cars. Then I had a job taking 'Stars in Battledress' artists around army camps. We stayed in different camps each night, in Nissen huts with a round stove in the middle. You only remember the fun times, but it must have been cold.

Then came another move, to Folkestone. I was issued with tropical kit. Goodness knows where we were going. Next came Liverpool and we boarded a large liner – we were told we were disembarking at Port Said transit camp, then Cairo, stationed in Kas-El-Wil barracks on the Nile. Now I could see the Grand Hotel that I had read about in the twopenny novels. I drove a bus that picked up civilians that worked in General Headquarters. My passengers worked for SSAFA [Soldiers' Sailors' and Airmen's Families Association].

One of our girls took sick and died. We were not allowed to visit her, as it was something infectious. Our company went to the funeral in a sandy desert cemetery.

Volunteer Underwood, a former laundry worker who joined the ATS, has her first lesson in driving a heavy army lorry from a Royal Engineer.

I sailed on the Nile in a small dinghy, visited the pyramids, the Sphinx and the museum – most of the treasures had been removed. I travelled and met lots of friends – not bad for someone from the Valleys.

'Aliens', as foreign nationals were known at that time, were not allowed to enrol at this stage – fears of spies known as 'fifth columnists' outweighed sympathy for refugees from Europe. Also ineligible for the forces were women working for the government; members of the Voluntary Aid Detachments on the staff of hospitals or with special nursing qualifications; women serving in the Civil Defence Air Raid Precautions scheme; and those who had qualifications or experience in scientific, technical and mechanical areas, or were skilled factory forewomen.

Each volunteer filled in forms, was interviewed by a section leader and had a medical examination. References were also taken up. Once the volunteer had passed through these initial stages and been accepted, she would as likely as not return home and wait until she was called up.

ATS Rates of Pay, 1939

Chief Commandant – 28s 8d per day (£1.43)
Senior Commandant – 19s per day (95p)
Company Commander – 11s per day (55p)
Junior Commander – 8s 8d per day (43p)
Company Assistant – 7s 4d per day (38p)
Senior Leader – 5s 8d per day (43p)
Section Leader – 4s per day (20p)
Sub-leader – 2s 8d per day (13p)
Volunteer – 1s 4d per day (7p)

Pay for volunteers who passed trade tests could be increased to 1s 10d (9p), up to 2s 6d (12½p) a day.

Free rations and accommodation were usually provided but where this was not possible, allowances ranging from 8s 9d (43p) a day for chief commandant, to 3s 8d (18p) a day for volunteers were paid.

There was tremendous debate and dissension over promotion. At one point, Ellen Wilkinson, Labour MP for Jarrow and later Minister for Education, asked the Secretary of State for War if he was aware that, if one scrutinised the latest list of ATS county and senior commandants, with one exception, no qualifications other than a title would seem to be necessary. She asked if a full list of the qualifications of these ladies could be issued. Sir Vivien Warrender argued – somewhat unconvincingly – that this predominance of titled women was little more than coincidence. He said that these positions were often arduous and unpaid and that a title had nothing to do with the appointments made. They might well be expected to be filled by promotion through the ranks of the ATS.

More accurate, perhaps, was the view of Dame Helen Gwynne-Vaughan, who remarked that when companies had to be formed, the best-known female in the district had to be selected as commandant and, in the class-dominated Britain of the 1930s, that was often a lady with a title. Dame Helen also commented, in response to the question, 'What chance has a domestic servant of becoming an officer?' that there was, 'Every chance, provided she is the right sort of person, a person who is a

A radio operator transmitting and receiving messages from her station directly underneath the anti-aircraft gun-site. (Associated Press)

born leader, one whom the others will follow, of high integrity and intelligence.' Confirming the worst, Dame Helen kindly added that one of the finest officers she ever knew was the daughter of a police constable.

Cosmetics were another initial source of controversy. Rules on wearing make-up were up to the local commandant, although Dame Helen advised that cosmetics should be inconspicuous and natural. In practical terms, red nail varnish was not acceptable but colours pale to the point of invisibility were – just about. Miss Ainsworth, Chief Commandant for Northumberland, declared, 'It won't do the country any good if we

"Just there. 15s. Whole head perm."

Cartoon by David Langdon.

turn out a lot of drab-looking girls. I prefer make-up.' In November 1938, however, Mrs J.H. Neill, the chief commandant in Sheffield, had initially resigned over the issue but then thought better of it and stayed with the service. These disputes and muddles were typical of the early days of the service.

Peacetime training comprised a minimum of ten drills a year and attendance at a special camp, for eight to fifteen days alternate years. Each drill involved at least one hour's training. Pay for attending camp for eight days was 31s (£1.55) for officers and 10s (50p) for members, and double that for a fifteen-day camp. All those officers and members who had attended at least ten drills a year were given expenses.

Inevitably, given the attitude towards women generally during peacetime and the Phoney War – from the initial declaration in September 1939 until the invasion of the Low Countries in spring 1940 – women in uniform were not taken very seriously. Typical of the tone of the time towards women volunteers was this report in *Picture Post* on the ATS's first 120 recruits, who lined up at Duke of York's barracks on 10 October 1938 and were drilled by four (male) sergeants – two from the Coldstream Guards, and two from the Grenadier Guards: 'They faced the 120 hatless women – Britain's blouse and skirt army [who] had parked their hats and coats, their fox furs and handbags in the mess room. Most of them

It is said that Tangee was an orange-based shade specially created to go with the khaki-coloured ATS uniform, although this may have been merely an advertising gimmick.

were wearing high-heeled shoes and silk stockings. After an hour's hard drilling they limped back to the mess room wondering if they could ever "make it".'

If a national emergency was declared, recruits who had not received their uniform – which was the vast majority in 1939 – were told to report to camp with a woollen cardigan, two complete sets of underclothing, two pairs of stockings, two towels, a knife, fork and spoon, hair brush, tooth brush, boot brush, polishing brush, spare pair of shoes and overcoat or mackintosh. At first, many women were issued with just a brassard bearing the letters ATS in blue on black. A small silver brooch of the same design as the cap badge was also issued.

When a place became available at a depot, the new recruit was called up. If she was lucky, in these early stages she would receive the full uniform of jacket and skirt, shirts and ties, pullovers, hats, shoes, stockings, gloves and underwear. But in practice, few had much more than the ATS brassard. Allowances were paid for toiletries, laundry and shoe repairs, the idea being that coming clear of deductions, pay was pocket money. Dame Helen Gwynne-Vaughan blamed the delays in processing recruits mainly on the continuing shortages of uniforms. In truth, Dame Helen herself had to shoulder some of the responsibility for that. In her drive to make the army see the ATS on equal terms, she insisted that requests for uniform should take their turn on the waiting list alongside men waiting for their full kit. She had a similar attitude to complaints that flooded in about the appallingly spartan accommodation. Her wider aim was a serious issue for the ATS at this time. The army would regard them as no more than volunteers or 'camp followers' and argued that as nurses and their assistants, the Voluntary Aid Detachment, were not covered by military law, there was no argument for the ATS to be treated any differently.

One immediate problem was that continuing difficulties with uniform and the awful conditions in much of the ATS accommodation were encouraging desertions and resignations. Women began to leave almost as enthusiastically as they had joined. In August 1940, the discharge rate was 26 per cent. By the following December, it had risen to 29 per cent. In the same period, desertion went from 0.19 per cent to 0.47 per cent. While uniforms and accommodation were the main complaints, homesickness and the strangeness of army life also played their part. As many recruits walked out in horror as in anger. The middle-

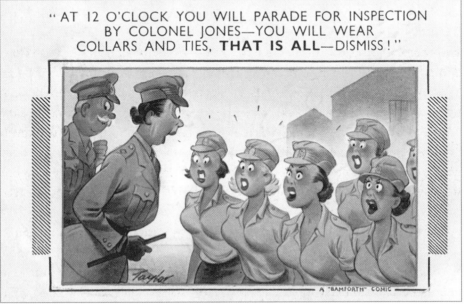

This very popular postcard needs no explanation and was still on sale in the 1950s. (Bamforth)

and upper-class girls and women who had been to boarding schools and in similar organisations were used to communal life. But those from lower-middle-class and working-class backgrounds, were often shocked and horrified by the lack of privacy, noise and bustle around them. Undressing and bathing in front of others was a completely new and unwelcome experience for them.

The rush to accommodate the ATS meant that recruits were often housed in totally unsuitable settings: one new barracks, a hotel in Kensington, had been condemned before it was taken over by the ATS. This only came to light after an apparent outbreak of measles among the women was correctly diagnosed as fleabites.

Meanwhile, the army was beginning to see that auxiliary forces could make an enormous difference to the course of the war. The government was investigating the shortfall in manpower in the armed forces and in the civilian defence services – and the shortfall was even worse than their most dire fears.

ATS Uniform

ATS uniform was based on that worn by the First Aid Nursing Yeomanry of the First World War and by the Motor Transport Corps. It comprised a lightweight serge khaki tunic and mid-calf, two-gore skirt. At this early stage, the material was of good quality – superior to that used for men in the army – and lined with khaki cotton. All the buttons were brass, of general service type. The tunic was mid-thigh length and was worn over a khaki shirt and tie. A half-belt was stitched on at the rear waist and the tunic had four buttons fastening to the right, in the male fashion – a suggestion of Dame Helen Gwynne-Vaughan herself, as this meant that service ribbons were worn on the left and would therefore be uppermost – and four pockets on the front; it also had two pleated breast pockets and two internal flap top pockets at waist level on each side. Epaulettes bore the legend 'ATS' in brass. ATS skirts were two-gore. The driving organisations pressed for shirts and ties instead of the cumbersome coat frocks of the First World War WAACs.

In the early years, members would wear the badges of their former organisation, such as FANY or MTC, on their sleeves after transferring to the ATS. This practice continued until September 1941. Slip-on cloth epaulette titles with ATS in black, and cheaper, printed versions were also used. Sometimes the titles were cut down to a disc shape and stitched straight onto the epaulette. Most of these variations were the results of attempts to kit out recruits in the face of mounting shortages of raw materials.

By early 1940, volunteers' main complaint was that they had to wear the uniform off duty so a new order allowed them to wear 'mufti' when on leave at home. Members could also wear civilian clothes while having their uniforms cleaned, and as Mabel Lethbridge observed in *Picture Post*, 'There seems to be a loophole here. If you want to wear mufti, you may happen to spill your soup.'

Officers received a grant of £16 towards their outfit. Uniform was issued free to others through county Territorial Army and air force associations. Mackintoshes, even supplemented with fleecy linings, were clearly inadequate so the greatcoat was essential. As more uniforms were produced, problems with one item, the greatcoat, persisted. Overcoats were in short supply generally and ATS recruits were supposed to have a fleecy lined raincoat instead. But these too were often difficult to obtain due to shortages.

By 1941, the sheer impracticality and limitations of the service dress became obvious as the ATS struggled and shivered in anti-aircraft batteries. Initially, auxiliaries on the sites had worn men's service shoes and battledress. By the end of the year, under its new director Jean Knox, battledress

ATS policewoman in uniform. (The Waverley Book Company)

*Peggy Wiggett in her ATS uniform
in 1943, at the age of twenty.*
(Peggy Wiggett)

tailored for women and special footwear of boots and gaiters had been introduced.
A voluminous fake-fur-look coat was brought in – officially labelled 'smocks A.A.
(wool pile) ATS' – and this came to be known as a 'teddy bear coat'.

By 1940 the ATS had 34,000 volunteers. Already in these early stages, the service
proved itself capable of far more than the official view originally envisaged. The
ATS was soon in action: some members served in France with the British
Expeditionary Force and some went over to Egypt in 1940. But a major problem
was that, as an avowedly voluntary organisation, the ATS was not subject to army
regulation and discipline. Penalties for disobeying orders were limited – dismissal
was the only penalty for military offences, hardly a deterrent in a case of
desertion, and other offences had to be dealt with in the civilian courts. ATS
members and officers could be discharged for a number of reasons, including
medical grounds, or at their own request, giving fifteen days' notice – except
during a national emergency, or because they had reached the age for discharge;

this was forty-seven for those in general service and fifty-five for those in local service. The practice caused considerable resentment, not least among male service personnel serving alongside ATS, but who were expected to bear the full brunt of military discipline for the same offences. So in April 1941, a defence regulation incorporated the ATS into the Army Act. Military nurses and other serving women were also included. Now, women had military status and were subject to full military discipline. ATS 'Other Ranks', called 'members' until July 1941, now became 'Auxiliaries'.

Dame Helen Gwynne-Vaughan was asked to retire on 21 July: she had been above the maximum age for enrolment in the ATS at the start but her job was done. Her abrasive manner, furious temper (often directed at her junior staff) and obsequiousness towards her superiors meant that her departure was greeted with relief by many, within and outwith the service. Her exit was an opportunity for an overhaul of people running the service. Despite official denials, Lesley Whateley, director of the ATS from 1943 to 1946, later commented that many of the ATS senior officers at this time were county ladies, who were in such positions only

Jean Knox, chief controller of the ATS, 1941–3. Her rank is shown by the badges on her lapel. (Bassano)

it's

time

I got a new hat

I always said I'd never join any of the Women's Services. Some sort of war-work, yes, but nothing that meant leaving home. Hated the thought of wearing uniform. Oh . . . lots of reasons. I was *quite* determined. Then I began to see those Government appeals staring at me in every paper I picked up. Telling me over and over again why I was needed in the A.T.S. It made me feel rather mean. ' At least I could talk to one of these recruiting officers,' I thought, ' they couldn't eat me.' And they couldn't force me to join either. And now I *am* so glad I went. It was like going to a college and choosing a career. I am going in for Radiolocation. That *is* a man-size job, with all a man's opportunities. The Cookery courses tempted me too. But there were dozens of good jobs, and I asked dozens of questions. I am looking forward to my new hat. Yes, I'm going into the A.T.S. to be part of the Army and help the men.

CUT THIS OUT AND POST IT TO-DAY

Address it to The Auxiliary Territorial Service, AG18 34i, Hobart House, Grosvenor Gardens, London, S.W.1.

Please send me full story of life in the A.T.S. and details of the opportunities it offers.

200,000

Mrs/Miss ....

Address ....

ATS

Age.........(in confidence). Age limits 17½ to 43. (Parents' consent needed under 18). Ex-service women may volunteer up to 50.
(Unsealed envelope, penny stamp)

urgently needed

You too, should take all your personal questions to the interviewing officer at any Employment Exchange or A.T.S. or Army Recruiting Centre. You will find her very sympathetic, and she will help you to understand what it's all about.

because of their titles. Dame Helen's successor was Jean Knox, a young and glamorous officer who was a deliberate contrast to her predecessor. During her two years as director of the ATS, Knox was conspicuous by her absence from many major events and meetings. Her contribution was nevertheless an important one: she smartened up the uniform, improved conditions and featured in a War Office publicity campaign that successfully gave the ATS a new image.

Leaving the ATS was now not so easy. However, a woman would be discharged if she were two or more months' pregnant under Paragraph 11 of the new regulations. For a friend of Anne Varley this was an obvious if drastic method of getting out: 'One of my mates was so determined that she crept to the men's quarters and shouted "Para 11" under the windows. She was hauled in within seconds and later obtained her discharge and an illegal abortion.'

In fact, few left the services although many disliked the jobs they were allocated and tried various means to change them, including feigning allergies encouraged by abrasive powder applied to the arms and

A recruitment advertisement stressing the chance to do 'a man-size job with all a man's opportunities'.

wrists. The more dramatically inclined would eat beetroot secretly – it turned urine red.

The following December, the National Service (No. 2) Act introduced conscription of women. Technically, conscription was a term used only for women sent into the auxiliary forces – those sent into civilian work or civil defence were termed 'directed labour'. Royal proclamations made single women and widows without children aged nineteen to thirty liable for service, although in practice, only those born between 1918 and 1923 were called up at first. They were given an option of women's auxiliary services, civil defence, jobs in specified industries or voluntary work.

Kitty Winfield joined at this time.

Actually I was in a reserved occupation – Post Office counter clerk – but I was keen to join the Wrens, which I was denied, as at that time – the early part of the war – one had to be the relative of an Admiral or similar to enter the Senior Service so I had to settle for the army.

In springtime '41 I was sent to York for basic training at Fishergate Barracks. Our first meal was cold corned beef and chips on a tin plate, an enamel mug for our tea. I soon settled down and made friends with girls from all over.

Kitty Winfield in 1941. (K. Winfield)

From York I went to Kenry House, Kingston in Surrey, for switchboard training in the Royal Signals. This was a lovely house which had been used by King Farouk when he was in England.

From Kingston I went to Reading. I think we were sent there until the army was ready for us on the Isle of Wight where we were sent to replace the men who were manning the switchboards and plotting tables in a gun ops room in Newport, as they were being sent overseas.

We worked in shifts, on the switchboards and plotting the hostile aircraft on a large plotting table (hoping all the time that the planes would never reach our homes).

In due course I volunteered for overseas service but was not able to go as my Mother was upset about it and wrote to the commander asking for me to stay in England. I was very disappointed. Later on the ATS were compulsorily sent overseas – I did not agree with that.

As Anne Varley recalls, 'The change in women's lives was extraordinary. For the first time, most earned their own money, controlled its expenditure and were free from the criticism of family and neighbours in so doing. Women had enough money to enjoy themselves as the war progressed; with their new friends, they visited pubs, attended factory and service dances and broadened their vocabulary to include not a few swear words.' The ATS soon learned to respond thus to soldiers who called them 'officers' groundsheets'.

Mary Bateman, then aged eighteen, joined in 1942 and was one of thousands of auxiliaries who went overseas:

In 1942, after thinking about it for many days, on April 30th, I volunteered for the ATS. I did it eventually on the spur of the moment, without telling anyone; needless to say Mum was rather upset. I had my medical and finally I was on my way during early May 1942. I made friends with a girl name Jessie Grant while we were gathered together on the station, waiting to be transported by train to a barracks near to Lancaster.

We were billeted in huts and had to do three weeks' basic training. We spent many hours marching around the barrack square. We learnt to salute an officer, stand to attention and at ease all to order, to halt quickly and smartly while we were marching, all the stuff that soldiers do. You closed your hand into a fist with the thumbs pointing to the front while you marched and swung your arms shoulder high. We were split into three sections with a competition at the end to see who was the smartest. I was in the swimming section; we also did route marches round the surrounding countryside which I quite enjoyed, having been a keen rambler.

In between we were issued with our uniforms and clothing, khaki-coloured knickers and thick stockings the colour almost of pea soup. We had quite a few injections against various diseases and a vaccination against smallpox.

One night they got us up in the middle of the night on a practice air raid alert. We had to don steel helmets and gas capes; goodness knows what I looked like, my gas cape was down to my ankles and my steel helmet wasn't a very good fit and kept slipping.

Finally we had a number of written tests and puzzles to do, to find out what they thought we'd be suitable to train for. I'd set my heart on being a teleprinter operator in signals. I was a typist in Civvy St, and I wanted to do the same job that my eldest sister Edie was doing, who was already in the ATS. The Army tried very hard to persuade me to go into ack-ack [anti-aircraft], which would have meant me being behind a gun shooting planes down. Not at all what I wanted to do. I finally won and was given a posting to a signals training unit at Upton near Chester.

I did another few weeks' training at Upton. This time it was all technical work learning to use a teleprinter and the phonetic alphabet – A for Able and suchlike. We thought it was all pretty wonderful stuff to be able to sit at a teleprinter and your message coming out on another teleprinter miles away.

At the end of the training we had to pass speed and accuracy tests.

I had asked to be posted to Chester, which was Western Command HQ (code name Westco). Edie was working there then and under army rules you had the right to be with a brother or sister. I got my posting to Chester but then found Edie had been posted to Burton-on-Trent!

At Chester I lived in an old college. I worked at Western Command Headquarters which was sited by the River Dee just the other side of the suspension bridge. I was in Chester for eighteen months with not a lot happening. I managed to get home sometimes and very often hitchhiked a lift. Life wasn't so hazardous in those days, and everyone gave lifts to service personnel. I sang a bit at that time, and we put on a concert in which I sang a couple of songs.

By mid-1943, twice the proportion of women aged fourteen to fifty-nine were enlisted in the forces, munitions and essential industries as had been in 1918.

Diana Williams, an ATS volunteer from British Guyana in the West Indies, retreading tyres at a depot in the West Midlands. By the end of 1943, over 2,000 people from the West Indies had come to Britain, most of them at their own expense, to volunteer for service in the three forces.
(The Waverley Book Company)

Nearly 3,000,000 married women were employed, compared to 1,250,000 before the war. Of those aged between eighteen and forty, 90 per cent of single women and 80 per cent of married women and widows without dependant children were in the auxiliary forces or in industry. From 1941 to the end of 1943, the ATS, particularly, underwent a huge expansion. By December 1943, it had over 200,000 auxiliaries and 6,000 officers in more than 80 trades. The range of tasks had expanded enormously as the national manpower shortages hit home. As part of the propaganda barrage, the 1943 film *The Gentle Sex*, co-directed and narrated by Leslie Howard, showed a group of women from a wide variety of backgrounds shape up into effective members of the ATS.

Jean Knox retired from the service on the grounds of ill-health in October 1943 although Lesley Whateley, deputy director, already regularly stood in for her on day-to-day matters as well as official occasions, including the celebrations to mark the ATS's fifth birthday one month before. Knox's efforts to improve the image of the ATS had been very successful. She had been assisted in this aim by a commission on the 'amenities and welfare conditions of the service', which published its report in August 1942. This commission, like the one set up during the First World War, had found, similarly, that allegations of immorality were unfounded. It also made recommendations for improving life in the ATS. Its work was widely made known and also restored public confidence in the service.

Lesley Whateley took over a force that, in her predecessor's short tenure, had increased from 40,000 to 204,000 members. She concentrated on improving morale which had, once again, begun to flag.

The spur to the ATS's rapid increase in personnel was necessity. Shortages of men in the armed forces meant two clearly specified taboo areas were now broken – first, women were firing guns (albeit discreetly on remote stations) and, secondly, women were working with men in mixed anti-aircraft batteries, directing searchlights to pick out enemy aircraft or guide their own planes home safely.

Refugees formed one of the smallest groups of volunteers

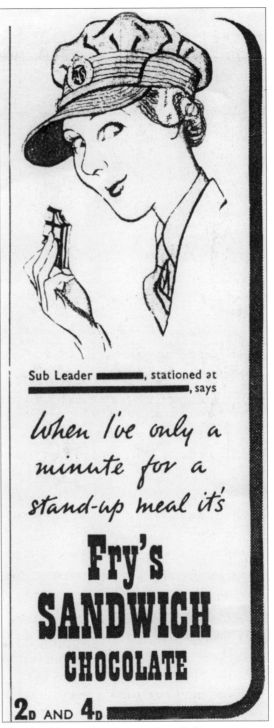

Sub Leader ▬▬▬▬, stationed at ▬▬▬▬, says

When I've only a minute for a stand-up meal it's

Fry's SANDWICH CHOCOLATE

2ᴅ AND 4ᴅ

A rather jaunty advertisement from 1943.

for the auxiliary forces and they were also some of the most committed anti-Nazis. Many, like Susan Lustig, a Jewish refugee from Germany, had a very much clearer idea of what they were fighting for than their British contemporaries:

About 9,000 men and 1,000 women joined the British armed forces during the war who were officially classed as 'enemy aliens', albeit with the contradictory qualification 'friendly'. We were refugees from Nazi Germany, about 60,000 of whom were in the UK when war broke out. 16 per cent of these volunteered for active service – a far higher percentage than in the case of their British contemporaries! I was one of these 1,000 women.

By 1943 even young people who were not British citizens were called up for war work, and my turn came in that year. I had arrived in this country in July 1939 – only a short time before the war broke out in September – and having been persecuted in Germany for belonging to an 'inferior race' (i.e. being Jewish), was at least as keen as my British contemporaries (if not more so!) to fight the Nazis. So when I was required to register for war work I chose to join the ATS rather than doing factory work, although pay for the latter would have been far better. Being non-British I was only allowed to do what was called 'general duties'. Specialist jobs like 'ack-ack' or driving were not open to us. As I worked as a dentist's chair assistant before joining up, I was at first attached to the Dental Corps, which counted as 'general duty'.

After about three months it was discovered that there was no establishment for female dental assistants, and I was sent on a four weeks' training course for medical orderlies in York. There I was taught how to bandage, give injections, and so on. However, to my disappointment I was unable to put these newly acquired skills to any practical use as my first posting was to Nottingham, where my duties consisted of de-lousing the hair of fellow ATS girls. The Army Post Office was located there, and the girls attached to it mostly had the long, permed hair fashionable in those days, which they did not like to comb out, and even less to wash! I was soon promoted to lance-corporal, but still felt frustrated about the work I had to do.

I was fortunate that by chance I met an old acquaintance who was also in the ATS when on leave in London, and she recommended me for attachment to the Intelligence Corps, where she was serving. After interviews at the War Office in London lasting a whole day – deemed necessary to establish my 'integrity' – I was accepted, and in the winter of 1943 I was transferred to a prisoner-of-war camp in Buckinghamshire, where immediately on arrival I was promoted to sergeant. This was an intelligence-gathering outfit in which all three services were represented – we had WAAFs and WRNS as colleagues, and men were there too (although the male other ranks were all army). I was very pleased to be able to do more productive work at last, and to put my knowledge of German to some good use. My work consisted of translating, typing reports and checking documents. It was extremely interesting, highly secret and confidential, and we felt that we were making an important contribution to the war effort. During that time I was further promoted to warrant officer II.

Shortly after arriving at this unit I met the man who later became my husband – he came from a similar background to mine and had been transferred to the Intelligence Corps from the Pioneer Corps, which at first was the only regiment that ex-German refugees were allowed to join.

As preparations for the invasion of Europe progressed, more and more auxiliary forces personnel prepared to go over with the fighting forces. Mary Bateman's skill as a teleprinter operator took her to the allied headquarters in Europe:

Towards the end of the eighteen months, I was on duty one evening, when the junior commander came wandering round watching people work. She came and stood over me. I was on a busy machine and I loved my work. I was a good teleprinter operator. Some nights later I was on duty again when I got called to the telephone and someone was asking me if I would go and work in London, to a new unit that was being formed there. I asked if I could have time to think it over, but no – they wanted an answer there and then. I didn't relish going among the bombing again but I was very patriotic then – For King and Country and all that! (Also I was surprised at being asked and not just sent.) So I said yes. It would have been the beginning of 1944 when I eventually left and went to London. We were housed in some old Regency type houses. Our place of work was underneath an empty gasometer. You could have put quite a few houses inside it. This HQ was named Rotunda, for obvious reasons, as the rooms all led off circular corridors.

They worked us very hard there, and we weren't very pleased to find out some time later that we were flogging ourselves to death sending out dummy messages, and it wasn't real work at all. We were told we were being brought up to scratch, in readiness for the future, which would be the invasion of France and Germany; we would be part of it. Everything was Top Secret. It was decided that some of us could help out doing night duty at the War Office, on their teleprinters so their girls could get a little sleep.

A lot of the work at Rotunda was sent out in cipher. Cipher was just groups of five letters that didn't exactly spell anything – for example, HZYGD or DNXRM, any combination of letters. Messages that came in, in cipher, went to a special office to be decoded into readable matter. It wasn't very easy to type, as it's not like spelling a word. We had to do a special test of 500 groups of cipher for both speed and accuracy. I'm blowing my own trumpet again, because no one else passed it with flying colours – me who didn't excel at school at all! I got my first stripe not long after that, making me a lance-corporal.

We moved from Rotunda to a base situated underneath Goodge St Underground station. We went down to that level, then descended further to our office. Train passengers must have wondered where we were going, but all the porters and ticket collectors must have known what was going on.

There was also a rickety old lift on Tottenham Court Road we could use. It was a terrifying thing, I think it might have been a lift that maintenance engineers used. It seemed to go down forever into the bowels of the earth. All leave was cancelled now.

Round about this time we were issued with our new arm flash to sew on our uniforms. It was lovely, very eye catching. It was shaped like a shield with a flaming sword up the centre and across the top was a rainbow. It was supposed to symbolise the 'Sword of Freedom' and the 'Rainbow of Hope'; and SHAEF was born – Supreme Headquarters Allied Expeditionary Force. We were all very proud of ourselves. I can remember being on a London bus, waiting to get off, and the conductor looking at my arm badge and saying, 'My, I bet that's weighing you down'.

A short while later our headquarters moved to a camp in Bushy Park near to Hampton Court Palace. This time we lived in army Nissen huts, run by the Americans. They shipped their own food over and we didn't go short of anything. I felt quite guilty sometimes knowing the rationing and shortages in the rest of Britain. We had PX [US forces] rations, the same as their troops. We were allowed about seven bars of chocolate a week, and as sweets etc. were rationed, we felt we'd died and gone to heaven!

One day we were called together and told we would be required one day to go overseas, so would we all please volunteer for overseas service (they didn't post girls overseas in those days unless they volunteered), otherwise we would have

Joan Ramsay (front row, third from left) at the camp in Bushey Park, Hertfordshire.
(J. Ramsay)

to leave the unit. It was blackmail really. We'd all come so far and done so much together. I don't think anyone refused. This meant we had to have some more inoculations including another booster dose which I was allergic to. I had to tell the American doctor I wasn't supposed to have it again. He gave me a test just under my skin. Sure enough I came up in a lump. I didn't want to be kicked out of the unit; I couldn't go abroad unless I had it done, so he finally decided to give it to me in small doses over the space of one and a half hours. I shall never forget it, because he kept singing a song from one of the Gilbert and Sullivan operas, *The Flowers That Bloom in the Spring Tra La*. He'd have a sudden burst of song and come and stick the needle in me again. I didn't have any bad reaction this time so he obviously did the right thing.

I was actually on night duty on the 5/6 June when the invasion began. Everything was coming through on the printers with Most Immediate as a heading. It was all in cipher and there was great excitement in the air. An American general visited us during the night and though the cipher office weren't allowed to say, we all knew that something big was happening. Next day it was impossible to sleep, for the steady drone of planes across the sky all day long.

Soon afterwards, the Germans hit back with the V1, known as the flying bomb or buzz bomb.

At our camp, we had a little Bofor gun quite near to us firing away at them, which meant we had to wear steel helmets as the flack from the gun was quite dangerous.

I took to sleeping under my bed. I couldn't sleep a wink on top of it. I used to put two 'biscuits' onto the floor to lie on and placed one at the top of my bed so it was over my head. I slept quite soundly like that. I'd even perch my steel helmet over one side of my head and still sleep. Fat lot of protection the bed would have been if a buzz bomb had hit us, but there you are – it worked for me!

I hadn't been home for at least seven months. I knew we would be going abroad in the not too distant future, and I wanted to see my family before I went. I could get a sleeping out pass, but wasn't supposed to travel very far on that. With doing shift work it wasn't very easy for authority to keep tabs on us. Someone offered to sign me in, so with the pass, it meant I could manage a couple of days. Very illegal and I'm not really the criminal type, so it was with great trepidation that I braved Euston station to catch a train to Manchester. If I had been stopped by the Red Caps (Military Police) I would have been in trouble. I was pleased to get home though it was only for a short period. It was coming up to my twenty-first birthday, and Mum had a cake made for me. I arranged a code with Mum and Dad so I could let them know when I went to France.

My twenty-first birthday was on 26 September 1944. The girls bumped me up and down on the washroom floor twenty-one times and we all had a piece of my cake. A few weeks later in October we were told to pack all our things ready for off.

I duly wrote my letter home and used my code to let Mum and Dad know when I was going.

The Americans were flying us over in small planes called Dakotas, fewer than thirty of us in each. The seats were in a row down each side of the aircraft. Our kit was packed all down the centre. We sat in the plane for quite a long time. Finally the American crew said the weather was too bad to take off, so we were taken back to camp. On the third day they flew us over.

The crew said we must be needed in France very much to fly us over in that weather. It was a dreadful journey, very rough. No sooner had we taken off than people started being sick and there were no mod cons. It was a case of 'Pass the bucket please'. One girl was so ill they had to find room to lay her down. The American crew were very kind to us. We landed on an airstrip just outside of Paris. It was a sea of mud, and we made a very bad landing.

Our new quarters were an old barracks in Versailles. I shall always remember seeing the Champs Elysee for the first time on that journey, a beautiful avenue, lined with horse chestnut trees.

According to many, however, the accommodation was far from palatial:

I still have nightmares about the toilets! They consisted of wooden huts built over a pit. Inside each was a row of toilets with a wooden partition between each one but no doors. They did eventually put curtains up for doors, but it was a long time after, it was all very smelly, and embarrassing. We called it the 'Rose Garden'.

We had said goodbye to our American friends before we left England. Now in France we were back with British Army methods and it really wasn't very nice. We worked in a building opposite the Palace of Versailles, and often used to walk in the Palace grounds. Of course none of the fountains were working, but the surrounding gardens and woodland walks were very beautiful.

Mary was in Paris on VE day, 8 May 1945:

It was a very emotional day and a bit frightening. The people just went wild. I've never been in crowds like that before, and don't think I want to be again. I was only 4 foot 11 and slim in those days.

Going back to Versailles at night was amazing. The train was so packed people were just hanging on the outside of it. A few weeks later, I was on a Victory Parade through the streets of Paris. Over 2,000 troops took part. It was quite an experience, because again the streets were crowded and people cheered us like mad. Every so often we'd be out of step; it was such a long parade and there were three bands. Then there would be a quick shuffle all round while we all got back into step again. I kept thinking how awful, whatever will people think of us? I don't suppose anyone cared two hoots or even noticed!

Morale received a late boost in 1944 when Princess Elizabeth (now Queen Elizabeth) joined the service – encouraged, according to Lesley Whateley, by the

Joan Ramsay (left) and friends at the Montgomery Club in Brussels. (J. Ramsay)

enthusiasm of the Princess Royal who was the ATS's Commander-in-Chief. Lesley Whateley had known the princesses since childhood but even so, she commented, 'I was absolutely staggered because we had all taken it for granted that she would go into the Navy as a Wren. I was also proud and honoured that they had chosen the ATS. Looking back on the dark days in 1940 when adverse criticism was our only form of publicity, I realised that this official sign of appreciation and confidence in our service was evidence of how it had improved.'

Princess Elizabeth joined the ATS in the spring of 1945. During her three-week training at the Motor Companies Training Centre at Camberley in Surrey, she learned map reading, maintenance and ATS administration. The king and queen paid an official visit, after which the princess remarked, 'I never knew how much trouble we give when we go to inspect anything. I must tell the king and queen what happens when they go visiting.'

When it was time to leave, Maud MacLellan, the chief commander at Camberley, said that the princess told her, 'I'd give anything I possess to be an ordinary person like some of my own friends and to be an ATS officer.'

By the end of the war, ATS casualties totalled 405. Of these, 67 had been killed in action, a further 9 died of their wounds, 16 were posted missing and 313 were wounded.

CHAPTER 3

Anti-Aircraft Command

By the start of 1940, anti-aircraft defences were short of 1,114 officers and 17,965 other ranks. General Sir Frederick Pile suggested women be deployed. As the officer commanding-in-chief Anti-Aircraft Command, General Pile had discussed the matter before the war and had asked Caroline Haslett, a well-known engineer, for her views. 'As a result of this investigation, she had assured me that women could man searchlights and fire control instruments and, in fact, do almost everything except fire the guns. As a matter of fact I could not see why they could not fire the guns too,' he said.

There was plenty of opposition to the idea that women should be allowed to do anything in the war that involved carrying or firing weapons. Even so, large numbers of ATS women were already deployed in other capacities on anti-aircraft work. General Pile remarked, 'I also knew what we were letting ourselves in for because I had already had considerable dealings with high-ranking ATS officers and their views and mine were rarely in tune.'

Despite his strong support for the ATS, the general felt that this situation had become unworkable. In those early days of the war, Anti-Aircraft Command was unique in the extent to which the work was carried out by the ATS. ATS women in Anti-Aircraft Command had access to vital war secrets and he wanted to put them into ops rooms where reliability was essential. General Pile's plan was for the ATS women working in Anti-Aircraft Command to become part of AAC rather than remaining in the ATS, as part of a separate, but linked, organisation. The ATS would not have it. 'The ATS were very jealous of their position. They were a women's service, run by women. No male officer should have authority over them nor was his advice needed. They were there to help the Army but only as they saw fit.'

A recruitment drive for ATS volunteers for anti-aircraft was redirected to attract specifically volunteers for gun-sites. Most notably, the 'teddy bear coat' and better footwear were introduced. And, Sir Frederick Pile advocated, 'as

ATS recruitment drives such as this one in Dundee emphasised anti-aircraft work. (HMSO)

women would be taking over identical jobs from men, they should receive the same rates of pay'. The plan was to replace 15,000 men with 18,500 women by the end of 1941. This would reduce the deficiency in manpower to 3,000. General Pile commented: 'It was pure mathematics that forced everyone's hand. With great anxiety and with prophecies of doom ringing in our ears, preparations were made for the beginning of the great experiment. The first mixed battery was to go into training in the spring. I should like to add that from the day Mr Churchill heard of the proposal he approved, and at once said that his daughter Mary would

Women who volunteered for anti-aircraft work receive training at a gun-site 'somewhere in England'. (Odhams)

be glad to join a mixed battery.' Before long, Mary Churchill was the junior commander of 481 Battery in Hyde Park, London.

By the start of 1941, more women were leaving the ATS than were joining and the number of new recruits was falling steadily too. At that stage, the service did not come under the Army Act and so ATS personnel were not subject to the same discipline as men in the army alongside whom they worked. Women could decide to go to other work and leave the service. Parents were a major influence. General Pile felt they were, 'always more of a nuisance than the girls themselves ever were, withdrawing their daughters at ten times the rate they had previously'. But the problem was not simply about a dangerous lack of urgency. Discipline and the discrepancies between the ATS and the army was a source of regular dissent and argument. 'I could not see why, if a woman was to play exactly the same part in a battery as a man, she should be controlled by a women's organisation such as the ATS (instead of the Royal Artillery). It was impossible, to my mind, to have two forms of discipline: one which told men that as long as they were back by 11 o'clock at night they were all right, and the other that said women must be safely in bed by ten. I wanted to make the women soldiers in the same way that the men were and to give them the appropriate ranks, Gunner, Bombardier, Sergeant and so on.'

One member of the ATS Directorate, whom collectively and individually the general blamed for blocking reforms, told him that unlike their male counterparts, women would be unsuitable for ack-ack because, unlike men, they might routinely smash valuable equipment because they would be so bored.

But by May 1941, the regulation bringing the ATS under the Army Act had been issued and Royal Artillery heavy anti-aircraft batteries had been formed with large contingents of ATS personnel. The ATS establishment grew rapidly, and most of the increase was in Anti-Aircraft Command: by the end of 1942, of 220,000 women enrolled in the ATS, 170,000 were in ack-ack. In August 1941, the first mixed battery was deployed in Richmond Park. General Pile said, 'It was as good as a visit to the Zoo. Crowds would assemble anywhere there was a site with ATS on it and stand and gaze in fascination. This was particularly true, a little later, of the all-female searchlight sites.'

Throughout the war the senior officers of the ATS and Anti-Aircraft Command continued to argue the extent and nature of the women's duties, despite the success of the mixed batteries operationally. In *Roof Over Britain*, the official history of Britain's AA defences, 1939–42, it was reported that the introduction of mixed batteries was 'not a whimsical experiment but a necessary operational plan. There are not enough men to go round now and as AA defences are almost continually increasing, the problem gets more and more difficult.' Women had 'the right delicacy of touch', were good at 'knob twiddling' and 'keen'.

In the mixed battery, women drove and serviced the trucks, acted as sentries and dispatch riders – did everything, in fact, except fire the guns. In the first mixed battery there were more than 200 women and nearly 200 men. Eleven male officers and senior NCOs from established batteries combined with three ATS officers to form the nucleus of control. Female officers concentrated on welfare issues and administration; male officers dealt with operational matters. If an ATS member needed to be disciplined, the male officer would report her to her ATS officer.

ATS rations were smaller than the men's but by mutual consent all rations were shared. 'Special regard was paid to the woman's need for fresh fruit, salads and milk foods; and a balance was found between this and the spotted dog and cheese and pickles so beloved of the old soldier – or the new soldier, for that matter.' (*Roof Over Britain*, HMSO, 1942).

Women in the operations room of anti-aircraft defences keep in constant contact with gun-sites.
(The Waverley Book Company)

In the late summer of 1941, the first mixed battery was sent to an operational site near London, once it had completed the three months' initial training. The first German plane to be shot down by a mixed battery was brought down in the Newcastle area on 8 December 1941. The officer commanding said, 'As an old soldier, if I were offered the choice of commanding a mixed battery or a male battery, I say without hesitation I would take the mixed battery. The girls cannot be beaten in action and, in my opinion, they are better than the men on the instruments they are manning. Beyond a little natural excitement which only shows itself in rather humorous and quaint remarks, they are quite as steady if not steadier than the men. They are amazingly keen at going into action, and although they are not supposed to learn to use a rifle they are as keen as anything to do so.'

The practical problem by now was accommodation. First were the difficulties in providing separate men's and women's sleeping and washing facilities, especially when set against a background of shortages in materials and labour. It was also true that what was considered acceptable for men in the army was, equally, completely beyond the pale for the women of the ATS. The head of the ATS described the accommodation in Richmond Park as 'disgraceful' and Sir Frederick Pile later complained that she had caused considerable upset among women on another mixed battery site by telling them that as members of the ATS, they could be transferred anywhere at any time because they were not part of the battery. This was actually true in theory, but in practice, breaking up a battery in this way would have destroyed it and was not likely to happen without good reason. It was simply too expensive in terms of staff, time and training.

It was also true in practice that the mixed batteries were outperforming even the highest expectations of their supporters. The key was thought to be in careful selection of personnel. Men in the mixed batteries tended to be older than average and preference was given to those who had worked alongside women in civilian life, rather than experienced army personnel who would find working alongside women in such a context more peculiar than most. Older men were picked because they were expected to look after the women – often teenagers – as they would their own daughters.

Before long, the ATS presence in the air defence of Great Britain became commonplace. When bad publicity surfaced, it was usually thoroughly countered by the new Public Relations Department which issued suitably inspirational photos of the ATS at work. For Sir Frederick Pile, 'The experiment has exceeded even my more sanguine hopes.' That mixed batteries outperformed all-male batteries was, he said, not surprising, given that those in all-male units tended to be low-category men, unlike the carefully picked soldiers in mixed batteries. As for the women, he commented, 'When the girls took to polishing their predictors, how could the men have dirty guns? And when the ATS sergeants paraded spick and span, could the orderly sergeant be less turned-out?' In spite of this predictable obsession with women's legendary abilities at housework, the general was equally driven to remark that in the Second World War, 'British girls were the first to take their part in a combatant role in any army in the world.'

Joyce Stott (née Baister) was stationed on several gun-sites around Britain:

I was a member of the ATS in a gun location team, which consisted of six personnel in telephone communication with a command post. You had to volunteer for the gun-sites, so though at twenty-six I was considered old for the job I volunteered and stuck out for radiolocation.

After kitting out, initial training and inoculations, the gun-site volunteers were sent to Oswestry for radiolocation training, theory and practice in operating. We were kitted out in battle-dress top, two pairs of trousers, two pairs of brown boots, one pair of brown leather gaiters, two pairs of socks, and a pair of denim overalls like a boiler suit for maintenance and fatigues. We

Two women working on a predictor. These two were part of the first wave of women to be drafted onto anti-aircraft gun-sites, often in remote parts of the United Kingdom. Apart from being cold and wet most of the time, women in anti-aircraft and searchlight batteries often worked under fire. (Crown Copyright)

were not allowed out of camp in battle dress, so kept the tunic, skirt, two shirts, shoes and stockings already issued to us in Harrogate. At one stage we were issued with long johns, but no one ever wore them, preferring the stockings which were quite thick though silky looking, under the socks. We wore a corset with suspenders and brassière. Our hands were protected from the cold – very necessary in the case of the girls on predictors and height finders and the spotters, as they were outdoors. All this was done by the stand-by team.

There were twenty-four gun location (GL) girls to a site divided into teams of six, each team having five operators under a corporal. When the guns went

These women at the range-finder on an anti-aircraft post are wearing the greatcoats issued from 1941 onwards as part of the major reforms in ATS uniforms, reflecting their wide, and increasing, range of duties. The famous 'teddy bear' coat was issued to women on operational sites from 1941. (Crown Copyright)

off we hadn't to jump as the predictor was following our dials and the guns were following the predictor. One team was 'on call', one on 'stand by' (we were unlikely to remain accurate after two hours). We were entitled to ten days' leave every three months.

After Oswestry our full team of twenty-four GL girls, together with gunners and ATS instrument operators, that is predictors, height finders, plotters, spotters, telephonists etc., were taken by special train to firing camp at Weybourne on the Norfolk coast. There the whole of the battery personnel were trained in seen and unseen firing techniques.

Our first gun-site was about 2 miles out of Reading. The worst raids were over, though we had several call-outs, being credited with one plane shot down. We were quite pleased to be told that the pilot had baled out and was taken prisoner – he was none too pleased to be told girls had shot him down.

Trials in August 1941 to determine the best way of coordinating searchlights and night fighters led to major changes in, and increased demand for, ATS personnel. Under the new arrangements, Indicator Zones and Killer Zones were created. Indicator Zones had lights spaced 10,400 yards apart, to show enemy aircraft entering the zones. In Killer Zones, lights placed every 6,000 yards would track an aircraft along its course. It was decided that from then on, fighters would circle round the searchlight and be directed to the enemy aircraft coming into their particular territory or Fighter Box – an area 14 by 44 miles around the light's vertical beam.

Many sites, therefore, needed only one searchlight where previously they would have had three, making thousands of searchlights available for relocation. As a result, the War Office demanded an additional 30,000 searchlight operators; implicit in this was the creation of all-female units. The opposition could point to a failed experiment along these lines in early 1941. But, once again, necessity brought about by the shortfall in numbers among male personnel

Toothpaste good enough for the services must be good enough for civilians. This advert from 1941 draws on the new role of the ATS on searchlights.

Spotlight on Service

Kolynos, the password to whiter and brighter teeth, renders a service to the 'Services–and to you too!

Sold everywhere in 3 standard sizes

KOLYNOS DENTAL CREAM
The Economical Tooth Paste

overcame entrenched opposition to expanding the role of ATS women. A major concern at the start of this second attempt was that many of the sites were in desolate and remote locations. Those stationed in such places would have to cope with loneliness. They also had to deal with intruders, even though they were still emphatically not allowed to carry guns.

As it happened, General Pile reported, 'We needn't have worried. . . . Considering the way in which they had been absorbed into the defences in other directions, I wonder that we ever did doubt that they would be able to carry out the job. And as for dealing with intruders, they showed themselves more effective, more horror-inspiring and more bloodthirsty with their pick-helves than many a male sentry with his gun, as several luckless and too presumptive gentlemen found to their cost, before the war was over.'

Generators for searchlights in these early days were not self-starting and so one of the better-kept secrets of the war at this time was the presence on these otherwise all-female sites of a solitary male solider whose job was to bring the heavy diesel generator into action. No politician – and therefore, presumably, no angry parent – heard about the moral turpitude these women faced.

By the end of 1941, the ATS comprised 170,000 members. Numbers continued to grow, and, the following year, the all-female 93rd Searchlight Regiment of the ATS went into action. At regimental headquarters there was the unheard-of phenomenon of a female adjutant. In the field, all the officers were women.

In May 1942, the first member of the ATS was killed while on active service. Auxiliary J. Caveney, of 148 Regiment, was hit by a bomb splinter while plotting her predictor at a site on the south coast of England.

Doris Legg (née Batley) was in D Troop, 495 Battery HQ, stationed at Horton, near Wraysbury in Middlesex:

In October 1942 I travelled to Harrogate in Yorkshire to become part of the ATS.

Doris Legg (née Batley) of 93rd Searchlight Regiment, D Troop, 495 Battery. (D. Legg)

Some of the girls were only seventeen and were quite homesick after a few days, but the older ones kept them occupied; they were a very mixed bunch, and soon settled down.

Everyone was interviewed and asked what they would like to do. I chose ack-ack, but we had to wait until the end of the course to know where we would be going. On the day an officer came along and read out names and places. There were just four of us left. He looked at us and said, 'Wait there a while, someone else is coming to see you. We immediately thought we were being sent home, and in our minds were already packing our bags. But we were told we were going to join the 'Elite' and would be trained to join the 93rd Searchlight Regiment.

My next destination was a searchlight training centre in Rhyl, North Wales, This was a very large camp of about 1,000 men and 300 women. It was a very lovely part of the North Welsh coast, but unfortunately the sea front was covered in barbed wire. A lot of our practical training was done at Kimnel Park, in Rhyl, North Wales, usually late at night, with a lonely pilot flying a small Avro Anson plane.

It was November and the nights were cold, but we were issued with boots, trousers, battledress tops and leather jerkins and later, when we were sent out to operational sites, fur coats with hoods.

A searchlight was a very large piece of equipment, and had many operative parts, all of which we all had to learn to operate. Each part had a number. No. 1 was the sergeant in charge; No. 4 operated the wheel that controlled the movement of the searchlight manually. Then there were Nos 6, 7 and 8, the radar operators. Their equipment was inside little tent-like structures, in which they sat and could control the searchlight by radar. No. 5 was the operator who threw the switch that actually put the beam into the sky. Then there was No. 9 who took care of the generator that powered the lamp.

The beam sent out an intense heat and a brilliant light. We were to learn how to keep this beam ready for action at any time an emergency occurred.

Besides operating the searchlight, we had to learn about plotting the course of the enemy aircraft. Plotting was another section of a searchlight regiment and was attached to some sites, but mainly at troop headquarters.

Some of the sergeants and corporals that took us through them in early training had come from sites that had already been taken over by the ATS. A few of them didn't think we should be doing operational duties, which seemed to us sour grapes because the ATS had been on the guns for quite a while. We were attached to the Royal Artillery and wore a small brass bomb on the breast of our tunics.

A member of the ATS serving in the anti-aircraft batteries. She wears the badge of the scales in black on a red background. The badge above the left breast pocket is the insignia of the Royal Engineers. ATS personnel often wore the badge of the unit to which they were attached during their time there. Wearing unit badges such as these was a privilege, not a right. (Author's Collection)

The radar tents on the equipment housed little screens that would pick up from the aerial any plane in the sky above. The operators could, by turning steering-type wheels attached, move the beam to where the plane was flying. They would shout 'on target' and the sergeant would respond 'expose'. No. 5 would then throw the switch and the beam would shoot into the sky.

None of that was difficult but maintaining the lamp was quite another story. The beam was actually run on carbons. These were like pencils and had to be put into the lamp housing so that one would lie straight along the top of the holder and the second one angled to the left and below the first one. When the switch was thrown the two carbons would strike together to form an arc and would burn for something like 20 minutes. Changing the carbons when they were in action was a very hot job indeed.

In February 1942, I left Rhyl for Windsor Great Park with nine other girls plus a sergeant and a corporal. It was a very good posting for me as I only lived 7 miles away.

A searchlight detachment is a very small unit and is made up of about 154 people housed in wooden huts. Outside the huts was the 'Lister', the generator that powered the lamp.

The searchlight was a few yards away from the huts and was connected by telephone to the radio telephone operator, taking instructions from headquarters. This was not a plotting site so my main job, apart from manning the telephone on night duty, was acting as No. 5 and being totally responsible for getting the lamp into the sky on the command 'expose' and getting it out quickly on the command 'douse'.

Thursday nights were 'barrack nights' when everyone had to clean everything thoroughly on site. Very boring except for one night when we saw the king and queen pass the site going further down the walk to inspect some cadets during their summer camp. We waved to them and they waved back. We were all wearing denim overalls and turbans on our heads – certainly not looking our best. About 30 minutes later, we saw them coming back and stood outside to see them. Imagine our surprise when the king's car stopped and they both got out. The bigwigs that were leading their car tried to get them to go back into the car but the queen insisted they came inside and looked round. They stayed about 10 minutes and the queen thanked us for allowing them to see how we lived.

Ivy Hopes, who spent most of her time in the ATS in anti-aircraft, seen wearing the white lanyard of the Royal Artillery. The usual ATS lanyard was of dark brown, tan and green but those in anti-aircraft usually wore the Royal Artillery's white lanyard. (I. Hopes)

After they left we told our HQ of their visit and were told off by our officer, who said not to play the fool on the radio telephones and she would deal with us in the morning.

One of the ATS top brass – Pamela Batten – came to visit us and of course we were sent a large tin of green paint to paint the searchlight. We argued that we could not paint it and get it dry in 24 hours. But our sergeant said 'they know that, so paint it and let it be on their heads if she gets smothered in paint'.

The great lady turned up looking very smart in her uniform and white gloves. We knew exactly what she would do and she did! She walked straight up to the searchlight and patted it. She said, 'lovely, you have done a great job', took off her gloves and handed them to her driver, who gave her a clean pair in return.

We worked very closely with our officers and got to know them very well. One of them was more than friendly with the major from HQ. It was a source of amusement to us because they always seemed to be arguing, she often in tears and we felt sorry for him, having her always phoning him, until one of his staff told us he was also carrying on with his ATS driver. We did not tell her, because listening in to their conversations was quite interesting.

Searchlights were also used as homing beacons. Many times bombers coming home from raids [had] their instrument panels damaged and so would have difficulty finding their way back to base. Searchlight sites for miles around would use their beam, by lifting it up and down and pointing it towards the air base to guide the aircraft home. From Horton we could watch the silver American Stirlings and the dark-coloured Lancaster bombers go out in the evening and come back in the early hours of the morning, often many of them limping home with part of a wing or an engine missing. Quite often not so many came back and sometimes we would hear a lone plane chugging across the sky and pray that he would make the last few miles home.

Each day a dispatch rider would deliver to us an envelope that contained the letter and colour of the day. This was the secret code that aircraft flying that day could use to avoid being mistaken for enemy aircraft. The correct colour flares would be dropped from the aircraft in the right sequence. If one envelope went astray the colours for the day would have to be changed all over the country.

By June 1942, the supply of ATS personnel was dwindling, as it competed with increasing demands for women from the other auxiliary forces and from the civilian services and industries. This affected the scheme to expand the searchlight regiments, now also sought-after for work overseas. Home Guard units were drafted in to help.

By 1944, the menace of the bombers had been supplemented by a new weapon, the flying bomb or V1, the first of which fell on England in June of that year. A few months later, the V2s – against which, in truth, no anti-aircraft measures were possible – were landing all over England. But ack-ack still had a job to do, especially in East Anglia, combating V1s launched from aircraft. In early 1944, Doris Legg was transferred to Isleworth: 'At this time Hitler was sending V2 rockets which could not be intercepted by fighters and could not be detected by radar. Searchlights were powerless against them. In October 1944, the nearest one dropped to our site fell at Ashford in Middlesex, which demolished two houses and damaged many more.' These attacks lessened by January 1945, although V1s and V2s were still being directed over the North Sea in the last month of the war.

The plan had been to replace mixed batteries with mobile units but the demand, especially overseas, for mobile units was such that the mixed batteries stayed where they were. This would have been all right had many of the ATS not been living in tents. The affair became a national scandal, especially when the Speaker of the House of Commons visited one muddy site during torrential rain. His report was glowing in its praise of the ATS, although he admitted to some bias because, 'I got rid of my civilian trousers at REME HQ, and put on battledress. I found on my return that my clothes had not only been dried but pressed as well. This was done by the ATS who looked after the domestic affairs of the mess. I have found the same wherever I have been – i.e. that provided the local ATS Officer in Command is the right sort, what women can do, both in the operational sphere and the more domestic sphere of running messes, is very great and no Victorian fears of the mixing of the sexes is justified by the tests of this war.'

Joyce Stott recalls: 'In early 1945 that we were moved to Ashford in Kent, or rather, to a farmer's field about 2 miles out of Ashford. There our accommodation was more primitive but the ATS still had their huts, each standing separately in a line, the ablutions being in a hut at the end with a boiler for hot water (only in the evening). The men, however, were in tents and had to take their showers in what looked for all the world like pre-First World War bathing machines drawn on to the site by lorries.'

The Home Guard, with whom the ATS worked on some sites, proved almost as effective as protective parents when it came to alerting MPs to the conditions in which the ATS carried out their duties. The problem was not just a need for accommodation: roadways, parade grounds, washing and eating facilities were also in short supply.

General Pile blamed the ATS's enthusiasm for, and pride in, showing they could 'rough it' in the same way as the men for unintentionally causing much of the fuss. The MP Tom Driberg asked questions in the House of Commons about the leaky tents in which some ATS were accommodated. Tom Driberg had been lecturing to some Royal Artillery men and had raised the issue as a result of conversations in the mess afterwards. The general assured the Secretary of State that this situation was no longer true, and had not been at the time the MP had raised the matter. A major building programme decided on in mid-October had been finished in just ten weeks. The men and women in Anti-Aircraft Command had successfully completed the project in a fraction of the time expected, laying roads, building accommodation such as sleeping quarters, mess facilities, entertainment and ablution blocks on the scale of an average-sized town.

Doris Legg remembers the last months of the war: 'Soon it was Christmas and then came the great news on 6 May 1945 that the war was over. There were great celebrations all over the country. There was no further use for searchlights, except that great night when most sites put their beams into the sky for the last time.'

CHAPTER 4

Women's Auxiliary Air Force

The Women's Royal Air Force (WRAF) was formed in 1918, on the same day as the Royal Air Force was created by the merger of the Royal Naval Air Service and the Royal Flying Corps. However, the WRAF was disbanded the following year and re-formed as the Women's Auxiliary Air Force (WAAF) in June 1939. Throughout the Second World War Katherine Trefusis-Forbes was head of the WAAF.

In *National Service*, published in early 1939, the government laid out the terms in which women were needed to assist the Royal Air Force:

Royal Air Force companies of the Auxiliary Territorial Service provide the opportunity for women to undertake non-combatant duties with Air Force Units in the event of war. The companies at present formed are for a) motor driving, b) clerical, c) general duties (cooks, waitresses, messengers and equipment assistants). The scope of the companies is likely to be extended to provide for the enrolment of teleprinter operators, fabric workers, upholsterers, photographers, tracers, and women for draughtsmanship duties. Enrolment will be for general service, i.e., within the United Kingdom or overseas, if necessary. The age limits are eighteen to forty-three years.

The Women's Auxiliary Air Force immediately took on 2,000 women who had volunteered for the ATS in the 1938 national recruiting drive. These women were in forty-eight ATS companies, attached to the RAF. Basic training for WAAFs took two weeks, after which recruits went into one of, initially, five trades. Within a very short time, however, the Battle of Britain meant that soon WAAFs were employed in a wide range of jobs, including aircraft and radar plotting; manning and maintaining barrage balloons; interpreting reconnaissance photographs; storekeeping and packing parachutes. WAAFs worked in communications and there were WAAF cooks and WAAF drivers. WAAF officers debriefed returning RAF air crews.

Many WAAFs worked in aspects of aerial photography, interpreting the results and, as here, maintaining the camera gun. This WAAF is in training at the school of instrument repairers and cine-projectionists. (HMSO)

Assistant section leader Daphne Pearson was the first WAAF to win an award for gallantry. In the early hours of 31 May 1940, a heavily laden bomber crashed onto the airfield near Daphne's quarters at RAF Detling. She ignored warnings from the guards and ran across the airfield, opening the gates for the following ambulance and fire crews. She told those already at the scene to break down the fence to give access to the crash crews, then climbed onto the blazing fuselage and brought round the unconscious pilot. As she freed him from his parachute harness and helped him away from the blazing wreckage, a 120-lb bomb exploded. Daphne shielded the pilot with her own body and when he was clear, went back to try and rescue the rest of the crew, but they were dead. The remaining bombs exploded. She was promoted to assistant section leader and awarded the Empire Gallantry Medal for her courage, the first gallantry award to be presented to a woman in the Second World War. She actually received the newly introduced George Medal. The reforms of 1941 meant that after this date, women were eligible for military rather than civilian gallantry awards, so Daphne was one of very few auxiliary women to be awarded a civilian medal. Dame Laura Knight, during that time an official war artist, painted Daphne Pearson's portrait, which hangs in the Imperial War Museum.

Daphne Pearson.

Official war artist Dame Laura Knight's portrait of Daphne Pearson. (Crown Copyright)

An early and frequently mentioned concern about women was that they might become too hysterical to be reliable in a crisis. In November 1940, after two months of heavy bombing, an unnamed WAAF flight officer addressed the point in a talk on the BBC:

I don't suppose airwomen on stations feel any different during raids from what ordinary people do in towns when they are bombed. If you've got a job of work to do you get on with it. Otherwise most people go to the shelters, except of course those who are on station defence duty.

You'll want to know which of the Women's Auxiliary Air Force are on duty during a raid. Well the switchboard operators for one; they are usually airwomen. Then there are first-aid workers, sick-quarter attendants, anti-gas squads and of course the plotters in the operations room.

Plotters particularly have proved that those members of the RAF were justified who said that women could be trusted to carry out operational work in air raids. They have shown they have plenty of nerve. So too have the telephone operators. Those WAAF who got the Military Medal this week were all telephone operators and it was a good thing they kept their heads and stuck to their job, because the station defence really depends a great deal on them.

As for the plotters I know one of them who had half a table where she was working bombed away, but she went on with her job. Two others had a shed blown down over them but when they were dug out they were still sticking to what they had been doing before the bomb fell. . . .

We rather like to feel, you know, that members of the Women's Auxiliary Air Force keep their heads in a crisis. We are proud to feel that we have been trusted to work in the front line, helping the RAF.

In *The Battle of Britain*, Richard Hough and Denis Richards record the often harrowing experiences of WAAFs listening to German and British pilots as they monitored radio transmissions over the Channel and southern England: 'One WAAF sergeant at Hawkinge, after reporting the regular appearance of a certain cheery-sounding German pilot on his Channel reconnaissance, then overheard the resulting interception by Spitfires, who shot him down in flames. "He was unable to get out and we listened to him as he screamed and screamed for his mother and cursed the Fuehrer. I found myself praying, 'get out, bale out, oh please dear God, get him out.' But it was no use. We heard him the whole way down until he fell below reception range. I went out and was sick"'

R/T monitors also knew when pilots were heading for disaster but could do nothing to stop it. In *The Enemy is Listening*, Aileeen Clayton records, 'They would hear a German leader yell the order to attack and know that he was diving on an unsuspecting RAF pilot below. I would often hear one of the WAAF operators murmuring, "oh God, oh God, please . . . *please* look up," and I knew how helpless she felt.'

WAAFs proved to be so good at plotting that from late 1940 they were transferred in huge numbers to the re-formed Royal Observer Corps (ROC). Originally, the Observer Corps had been run by volunteers, many of whom were men too old to be on active service. It had been so effective during the Battle of Britain in the summer of 1940, that it was renamed the Royal Observer Corps. But as the allies increased the size and frequency of bombing raids over Europe, the corps needed radical revision to track the vast numbers of planes – allied and enemy – flying back and forth to bomb each other's cities. An overall aim was to integrate the corps more closely with the Royal Air Force. Uniforms became compulsory and officer ranks were introduced. The procedures for plotting and telling were completely overhauled. At the same time, male members of centre

WAAFs plotting the course of a bombing raid. Most wear the overall or working dress. The latter was worn over the shirt, as seen here, or without. It might also be worn over the WAAF skirt or trousers. None of the women have hair touching their collars; with one exception (bottom row, fourth from right), all have long styles, pinned up. (Imperial War Museum)

The glamour of the WAAFs was called on to sell distinctly unglamorous Bile Beans. The strap of the WAAF's gas mask case is clearly visible and in the background, barrage balloons fill the sky. (Author's Collection)

crews over the age of fifty were compulsorily retired, and women were admitted to the corps for the first time.

Eric Wilton was a member of B Crew of the Royal Observer Corps centre in Bromley, Kent, throughout the war. He commented in his memoir that the compulsory retirement of every man over fifty caused enormous dissent. When the ROC crews pointed out the shortages this ruling would create, the rather tactless official response was that they should employ women in sufficient numbers. Eric remarked:

In view of the unquestionable efficiency of the women observers who ultimately formed about a third of the observers at Bromley centre; in view of their truly amazing courage during the nerve-wracking period of the flying bombs; and having in mind, perhaps above all, the increase in comfort and social well being that their presence brought into the centre, it was unfortunate in the extreme that their original entry into the corps should have thus coincided with the forcible expulsion of many of the best-respected and most popular of the original members.

The implied suggestion that a woman, possibly directed against her will, would make a better plotter than a man of fifty who had voluntarily sacrificed his few hours of leisure to serve his country, augured ill for the popularity of the new recruits.

[As things turned out] . . . when the first women recruits did arrive on the scene, their charm and tact quickly disarmed all possibility of criticism. Very soon, the most embittered misogynists (and we had some in B Crew) were forced to admit there might be something to be said for women plotters.

It was early morning of a dismal day in February 1943 that the first two female recruits appeared in B Crew. Their ordeal might have been severe and the weather and the time did nothing to lighten it. Anxious as every male observer was to welcome them, to make them feel at home, no one could quite escape the feeling that their presence in that sacred room betokened a leap into the unknown . . . one had grown used to women in business; one had become resigned to women in golf clubs; but here in the Observer Corps! Well there they sat . . . two small lions in a den of Daniels. . . . Mrs Field, very quiet and clearly ill at ease, and Mrs Godlee, talkative and apparently the reverse of embarrassed to find herself in so exclusively masculine a company.

A Man's Job

This contemporary postcard is in the style of Mabel Lucie Atwell. On the back is printed the message, 'NOW IS THE TIME FOR EVERYONE TO STAND TOGETHER AND HOLD FIRM! – the Prime Minister'. (Raphael Tuck)

Mrs Field and the men need not have worried. 'In a very short space of time the women observers were dovetailed smoothly into the social and operational structure of the Crew and life proceeded exactly as before, or almost exactly.' Eric described a typical night in July 1944, plotting V1s:

Almost at once, the first sound trumpet goes on Bromley table. It takes the doodle-bug no time at all to cover the few short miles between the coast and Bromley's boundary. The girl plotter on R. Posts – she looks no more than seventeen but self-contained, supremely confident – adjusts her headset and feels in the tray for a green counter. There is the drone of voices from the tellers as the counter goes down.

'Hostile Diver one zero four.'

'Roger 1761.'

'One at two.'

Apart from the monotonous voices of the tellers, the room is intensely quiet. The plots go down quickly. Three more green counters appear in quick succession. Four tracks are moving steadily across the table, green counters succeeded now by blue, blue leading into red.

'Diver 104 seems to be coming our way.'

'Roger 0373.'

'Queenie eight nine eight five.'

That line will bring him bang over the Centre. Already the heavy throb of his propulsion unit, with its curious overtone of urgency, can be heard clearly above the noises of the room.

'Queenie eight seven eight five.' The noise is deafening now. The plotters work on with calm, absorbed faces. There is only one thought in the room, though no one betrays it: suppose he cuts . . . some day if this goes on, one is bound to cut at just the right, the unlucky place. . . . Another plot goes down. Overhead at Centre. We hardly need a Post report to tell us that. The walls vibrate. The air in the room seems to throb. He must be terribly low. Sometime they don't cut. Sometimes they just dive headlong with the engine racing . . . stupid to think about that. If it comes, it comes.

This is not, after all, the one. Slowly the vibration lessens. The plotters exchange significant glances across the room. Tension has dropped from the room. Norman, the table supervisor, permits himself a heartfelt 'phew'. 'Another one for Forest Hill,' he says. Norman lives at Forest Hill. Almost before he has spoken, the throbbing drone abruptly ceases. A plotter calls 'Cut!' She places a crash counter beside her plaque. There is a dull, heavy roar. The building rocks unpleasantly. Somewhere a slate falls. Norman leans over the table and moves the crash counter to the point of intersection of the sound trumpets that have appeared like a rash on the circles of a dozen posts. 'Looks like Penge,' he says laconically.

By the end of 1943, WAAFs made up 16 per cent of the RAF's strength and 22 per cent of Home Command; 182,000 WAAFs worked in 75 trades with 22 officer branches. Many were on remote and sparsely populated stations, plotting radar or running barrage balloon sites. Women worked initially as balloon fabric workers and in the first months of the war, no thought was given to them

Mooring a barrage balloon.

extending their duties beyond this. Their usual tasks included sewing and repairing the barrage balloons and 'doping', the name given to mending tears in the fabric with a special pink glue. Barrage balloons, made of rubber-proofed cotton, weighed about 550 lb and were fixed with a flexible steel cable. They were filled with hydrogen, which expanded according to temperature and atmospheric pressure. Inflated, they were about 63 ft long and 31 ft high.

In the middle of January 1941, the air officer commanding, Balloon Command, was asked to consider using WAAFs for flying barrage balloons. Once again, the spur was the difference between the numbers needed and the numbers of men available. The magazine *Picture Post* reported positively on the experience of the first female barrage balloon crews: 'At first, this suggestion was received with some dismay. The fact that the manning of the balloons for 24 hours a day, frequently in the most appalling weather conditions, required physical strength not generally possessed by women, was considered in itself sufficient reason for rejecting it. . . . . The air officer commanding considered every aspect of the problem – physical, suitability, the accommodation the WAAF would need, type

*At the controls of a winch lorry,
used for raising and lowering the
barrage balloons.* (The Waverley
Book Company)

of clothes and food to be issued; the strength of WAAF crews, to whether they
should use lethal weapons.'

One month later, an experimental batch of WAAF crews – all volunteers and
mostly balloon fabric workers – were posted to the largest balloon training centre
in the country for ten weeks of intensive instruction. They trained under
eight RAF balloon operators, and spliced rope and wire, studying the sixteen
different kinds of cordage lines and rope and fourteen different knots. The
trainees also learned how to keep balloons in the air, how to haul them down, how
to repair damage to the fabric and how to stow them in the hangar. The operation
of the winch was the most difficult part of the work. The only job the women
could not do was hauling the hydraulic cylinders that filled the balloon. At the
end of their training they carried out a number of simple balloon operations
watched by a group of senior RAF technical and medical officers.

The air officer commanding told the Secretary of State for Air that the training
had gone so well that the women would be taking over from airmen on balloon
sites in a few days.

In 1942 volunteers were called to work as balloon operators and these trained with the RAF. The plan was extended to cover a large proportion of balloon sites. Training was slightly different – women, it was discovered, learned very quickly from models, so miniature blimps, sandbags and hangars and sites were made. Men learned more effectively from charts and diagrams. Other differences included painting the women's classrooms green and allowing the WAAFs to cultivate gardens round their huts.

Picture Post thought it necessary to point out that:

The substitution of WAAF for airmen on balloon sites does not imply that the airmen who have operated under all weathers and under aerial bombardment, have in any sense been doing a woman's job. In the first place, it requires a crew of 16 airwomen to replace 10 airmen. Secondly, RAF crews are incorporated into military defence schemes, whereas WAAFs are not. Thus, in a number of areas, it is not practicable for WAAF to take over sites. Lastly, it is only the great progress in and simplification of balloon manipulation, for which the original officers and airmen of Balloon Command are responsible, that has made the substitution at all possible. Skill and intelligence will still be required but the constant physical strain which was present in the past has been very much reduced.

The report adds that just as the RAF often called their balloons by girls' names, so the first WAAF crew to operate in London named their balloon Romeo.

As with anti-aircraft batteries, many barrage balloon sites were soon run entirely by women. Enid Burns was a WAAF officer at RAF Norton between 1941

A snowy day at Barrage Balloon Site 26, in Middlesbrough, Cleveland, January 1942. Left to right: Moll Brown, Jane Carnian, Vera Granger, Ronnie Nary (later Veronica Tournay), Phyllis Priestly and Babs Hammond. (V. Tournay) and 1942, in charge of WAAFs at three sites in the Sheffield area. 'These balloon sites were manned entirely by WAAF and it is thanks to them that many Sheffielders and steelworks were saved from enemy bombers. The balloons were used to protect the industrial heart of the city, not to protect civilian suburbs. They were a splendid lot of women – tough, brave, uncomplaining and cheerful, doing a very dangerous job as the winder and steel hawser were lethal and many accidents occurred. We also had a terrible fire in a hanger when a balloon was being repaired and the hydrogen ignited. Many WAAF were badly burned.'

Pamela Smailes was also based in Sheffield at a barrage balloon site:

One particular time a big flash car drew up driven by a corporal. A wing commander got out and was going to go on site. I was on guard duty and so I stopped him and asked for his identity card. He was angry but I would not let him go a step further. Our Sarge came over and was going to let him in but I was firm and said we would have to contact headquarters. Just then another car came down, full of officers. We were congratulated for being the only site to query their identities – they were checking up on our efficiency.

Site 20, 'C Flight', at Wincobank in Sheffield. Back row, left to right: Corporal Hayes, Kaye Mayhew, Janet Nichol, Pat Dunn, Dot Stark, Ruby Morton; front row, left to right: Edna Singer, Pamela Smailes, Corporal Barnes, Sadie Fawcett. (P. Smailes)

I had my leg pulled but as I said, it could have been a German. Anyway we got an award and were the envy of the other sites for the praise we received.

Not long after, the barrage balloons became obsolete and I was remustered as an instrument repairer but I shall never forget my time as a balloon operator.

In 1941, Hilda Pearce was on another all-female site, in London. 'We were based in Grosvenor Gardens and with all the trees around it was quite a hair-raising experience getting the balloon off the ground. The Marines from the American Embassy were very helpful and would come and pull on the ropes if they saw we were having trouble. Believe me it was tough. We had to do guard duties all through the night, 2 hours on and 4 hours off. We worked in the snow and rain but the wind was worst of all. If it was windy, we had to be pulled out of bed in the middle of the night every time the wind changed to put the balloon's nose into the wind.'

Anne Allibone (née Walder) was one of many working with allied forces stationed in Britain. Her son, Tom Allibone, recalls:

For most of the Second World War, my mother served with the Women's Auxiliary Air Force or the WAAFs at numerous RAF stations around England. She was assigned to the MT (motor transport) section and towards the end of the war and while she was stationed with RAAF 460 Squadron operating Lancasters out of RAF Binbrook, the Australian Prime Minister, John Curtin, visited.

He had come to see 'G' for George, the by-now famous Lancaster which had survived an enormous number of sorties over enemy Germany. On this occasion, my mother or 'Blue', as was her appointed nickname by the Aussie crews, was assigned to drive the RAAF (Royal Australian Air Force) officer selected to accompany the PM for a personal tour around the aircraft.

On the short journey out to dispersal, the officer, clearly rather nervous about his public relations assignment, confided in my mother saying, 'Do you know, Blue, I haven't a clue what to tell him about "George", I know so little about it!', to which my mother suggested that it might be a good idea to parry any of the PM's questions about the aircraft by saying that it is equipped with highly secret gadgets that cannot be discussed nor revealed to anyone, not even the Prime Minister of Australia. Some time later, my mother collected the somewhat relieved looking officer who, upon getting into the staff car said, 'Well Blue, there sits the most secretive aeroplane in the air force!'

Numbers in the women's forces, like the male equivalents, were boosted by the arrival of tens of thousands of volunteers from overseas. Aircraftwoman Mildred Davis of the Royal Canadian Air Force was one such recruit. Formerly a nursery nurse, her wartime role was as an MT (mechanised transport) driver.

WAAF Rank Structure

WAAF	RAF Equivalent
Commandant-in-Chief	Air Marshal
Air Chief Commandant	Air Vice-Marshal
Air Commandant	Air Commodore
Group Officer	Group Captain
Wing Officer	Wing Commander
Squadron Officer	Squadron Leader
Flight Officer	Flight Lieutenant
Section Officer	Flying Officer
Assistant Section Officer	Pilot Officer

WAAF UNIFORM

The service dress for WAAFs, authorised in March 1939, was based on that of the ATS, but in RAF blue. It had the black peaked cap and integral waist belt equivalent to the RAF's service dress. But whereas the male service dress was made from the usual rough serge, the female version was made from barathea

*Jonathan Foss's recruiting poster. The 'A',
just visible under the WAAF's albatross
'wings', stands for Auxiliary.* (Crown
Copyright)

(a wool and silk mixture), although wartime shortages meant this was replaced in time by wool serge.

All WAAFs wore the RAF albatross badge, and before 1941 most wore beneath it the letter 'A' for auxiliary. The standard RAF cap badge, with the letters 'RAF' surrounded by a wreath and topped by a crown, was worn on the front of the cap, on an open-weave black band. WAAFs wore a black beret on barrage balloon sites, and for dirty work. This was worn pulled down at the back and with the badge placed centre front. They also wore black wellington boots.

For some time it was thought that WAAFs' limited duties meant that they did not need greatcoats. Many women in uniform were extremely cold, as the range of duties extended far beyond official awareness and imagination in the chilly winter of 1939/40. Eventually, in November 1940, the WAAF other ranks' greatcoat was introduced.

Working suits of serge blouse, similar to the male uniform, and trousers were essential and were issued from early 1941. As with the service dress, a blue shirt and black tie were worn underneath the blouse. The Utility version of the working suit cut down on materials and labour costs. Brass buttons were replaced with black plastic. Unusually, the pleated pockets and three pointed flaps survived.

Officers' dress followed closely the style of RAF officers. It fastened on the right (men's) side. The light-blue-on-black rank laces of WAAF officers followed the patterns of RAF officers, on the lower sleeve. WAAF auxiliary officers wore the gilt 'A' on both lapels, as the equivalent of the other ranks' cloth badges. The gilt 'A' was also worn above the rank lace on the shoulder boards of the officer's greatcoat.

The officer's pattern of cap had a three-section crown and a cloth-covered stitched peak. The badge of the service dress cap was the same as that of the RAF officers – a king's crown above a gilt albatross, over a bullion wire wreath.

The shirt was in light grey-blue cotton. Each WAAF was issued with three shirts and six detachable collars secured by metal or plastic studs.

One-piece overalls, in dark-blue heavy cotton, were an alternative form of working dress. WAAFs had wrapovers equivalent to the ATS, but in blue, and cooks had white versions. Kitchen workers wore clogs in black leather, with leather patches on the wooden soles to prevent slipping.

WAAF personnel were posted overseas from 1940 onwards and in 1944, a khaki drill (KD) uniform was issued. This comprised a long-sleeved shirt bush jacket, slacks, skirt and the inevitable khaki stockings. The bush jacket was made from light cotton.

WAAF officers displayed their rank laces on KD epaulette slides. On postings overseas, officers from all the services often had uniforms with short sleeves made by local tailors. Sidecaps in air force blue were standard issue to WAAFs in the tropics from early 1944.

Nancy Furlong volunteered for the WAAF in 1944. Her decision was based partly on the persuasion of a friend already in the service, partly because her older brother was in the RAF 'and also, fashion-wise, I thought that the blue-grey uniform would suit me better than that awful khaki which the ATS wore'.

The uniform was made of good warm materials, a skirt which had a large back panel and front and two smaller panels each side. The smaller panels would be creased to the inside and the front and back seams very well pressed, rather like a brown paper carrier bag is folded. Using a sewing machine I top-stitched these four seams so that they stayed crisp without so much ironing. But on Pay Parade, we had to assemble before the officers and when your name was called you stepped forward, saluted and gave your number (mine was 2120847). After the parade, the sergeant called me into her

In peacetime, foreign travel was a luxury limited to the well-off, but wartime gave many more the opportunity to see the sights. Doreen Bradley (née Thompson) joined the WAAF. (D. Bradley)

Doreen was posted overseas to Egypt where, off-duty, she visited the Avenue of the Sphinxes at the Temple of Karnak. (D. Bradley)

Doreen also joined in concert parties. (D. Bradley)

office and said, 'The officer wants to know if you have stitched the seams of your skirt' to which I replied 'Yes', and was told to unpick it. I warned the sergeant that if I did it would fall to pieces. It did, so I had to have a new skirt, which I promptly restitched and pressed. The officers were not pleased if our uniforms looked well tailored like theirs.

On the tunic, I later unpicked the top-stitching on the pockets, etc. and hand stitched them. My main inspiration for this was a fellow WAAF who was the camp tailoress and she had modified her uniform in very subtle ways so that it looked like an officer's.

When you see the WAAF uniform, which is supposed to be authentic, on television, the cap is a dead giveaway. Usually it is shown with the top material all puffed up. We hated that effect so to make sure it kept flat, we would press it with a damp cloth then lay it down on the brim and inside uppermost and our steel helmets put on top to weight it down for a more streamlined effect.

The shirts we had were pale blue with separate collars. If you were lucky enough to be stationed near a Chinese laundry, the collars would be taken there and collected next week so starched and ironed that they were like celluloid.

These two women are, left, leading aircraftwoman M. Harvey of Hampton Court, Surrey, and, right, leading aircraftwoman J.M. Hayhurst of Manchester plotting the course of flying bombs sent from northern France. LA Hayhurst wears the insignias of wireless operators: a fist clenching bolts of lightning. These two are wearing the battledress trousers and tunic preferred by many WAAFs, given the chilly and often hard physical work many routinely undertook. (Kent Messenger Group)

Our stockings were blue-grey lisle held up by a pink suspender belt. Knickers, dark navy (passion-killers), and cotton bra. One of my friends was so amply proportioned that she had to go to Spirella to have her bras specially made. Black leather shoes and they, together with the brass buttons on the tunic, had to be polished every day. Woollen gloves, a navy fabric shoulder bag for our personal belongings. A big heavy overcoat – for which we were most grateful.

We were expected to keep it all in clean good order and most of us did. They were all the clothes we had and we were not allowed at that time to wear civilian clothes. One evening each week was domestic evening and we were not allowed out of the camp. We had to clean and polish our bed spaces and the one stove in the middle of the hut would be black-leaded. Our lockers were tidied and this was when we bundled and labelled our laundry such as sheets, towels, did our hand-washing, ironing and any repairing and darning to our kit. An officer would make an inspection and we quickly learned to dust the top of the doors. This seemed to be the standard test to try and catch us out.

Betty Sharp, newly commissioned officer, first left, back row. (E. Sharp)

Betty Sharp volunteered for the WAAFs in the late summer of 1941:

I was instructed to report to the Recruits Depot at Gloucester on 5 October. At the Medical Inspection hut we had one of the very frequent medical inspections which were known as FFIs (Free From Infection). These inspections were held whenever an airwoman was posted from one station to another. They were intended to reduce the spread of infection such as scabies and head lice. My first experience of the FFI was, to say the least, rather disturbing. We were examined by a WAAF medical orderly for skin infection or head lice and anyone she felt required treatment was told to 'stand over there'. To my horror, I was told to 'stand over there'. I have always been troubled with dandruff and I suspected that this was being mistaken for nits and in spite of my protests I was told to sit and wait. Eventually we were taken to another medical hut for treatment. Of course, by now I was fuming, and after the orderly had another look, she agreed that I had been sent there in error.

We were only at Gloucester for about a week and during that time we were given a broad idea of service life. We had numerous interviews by officers and they assessed our ability and decided which trade we were to follow. My trade was to be Clerk, General Duties.

After a week at the Recruits Depot we were all posted to Morecambe where we were to finish training. On the day we travelled from Gloucester we were to parade at 5 a.m. Before we left the camp each of us was issued with what was called 'the unexpired portion of the day's ration'. I think about 100 of us travelled to Morecambe and I heard that we were the second batch of girls to be posted there.

We must have looked a moth-eaten crowd because we were not yet used to marching and had no idea of keeping a step or halting at the right time. However, after some time, the squad I was with halted outside a house where some of us were to live and seventeen of us were taken inside. It was one of those terraced houses you get in a seaside town in what appeared to be a typical boarding house area.

We were all very keen and there was a great deal of competition between the squadrons as to smartness on parade. Batches of recruits arrived from Gloucester continuously and there must have been hundreds of WAAFs in training at Morecambe at one time.

While Betty was at Morecambe, the Air Ministry announced a major increase in WAAF establishment.

A large number of officers would be required. All recruits were to be interviewed with this in mind and some of us earmarked as 'officer material' and we went from one interview to another. Our training went on as before although occasionally we were detailed to help the NCOs.

I was posted to 16 Balloon Centre Sheffield. When we arrived, no one seemed to know who we were or what we were supposed to be doing. We felt most deflated. But this was one of the things we would get used to – suddenly out of the blue one would be posted most urgently to do a particular job and when one arrived full of enthusiasm no one knew you were coming.

Anyway, we soon settled down and after a while quite enjoyed the routine. I was in a hut with about thirty-two other airwomen. The complete lack of privacy was very trying but there was a good deal of give and take.

After several weeks, some of us were told that we should try a trade test. If we passed, we would be upgraded to leading aircraftwoman (LACW). Apart from a bit of a status symbol, this would give us an increase in pay. So we swotted up all the rules and regulations and general office routine and all of us

Yes, the W.A.A.F. still needs more recruits. It's growing in pace with the R.A.F. and when you join, an airman is freed for other duties. It doesn't matter what your job was in civil life. There are 48 different jobs you can do in the W.A.A.F. including Radio Operators, Plotters, Drivers, Clerks, Cooks and Orderlies. You'll be trained for the work that suits you the best. Don't hang back because you feel the W.A.A.F. only wants experts   It can soon make an expert out of *you*.

Enrol at once.   *The age limits for all trades are* 17½ *to* 43 *with few exceptions, or* 50 *in the case of ex-service women.   Go to the R.A.F. section of the nearest Combined Recruiting Centre (address from any employment exchange) or fill in the coupon for illustrated leaflet giving full particulars.*

To Air Ministry Information Bureau, Kingsway, London, W.C.3. *Please send me full details of service with the W.A.A.F.*

NAME ....

ADDRESS ....

By 1941, recruitment advertising placed heavy emphasis on training for a worthwhile job.

passed. However, by now my trade was no longer clerk, general duties but admin., so I was not able to sew the LACW badge – a propeller – onto my uniform. This was a great disappointment to me. I was now moved into the WAAF administrative office, given a trolley and all sorts of jobs to do. Among other things, for a time I was put in charge of shoe repairs for the camp.

In December a notice came from the Air Ministry that I was to attend a commission board. The senior WAAF officer told me what to expect but I must say that I felt very inadequate as I went into the Air Ministry in Kingsway in London for the interview.

There must have been six or eight WAAF and RAF officers on the board sitting behind a highly polished table. They put their questions one by one. They had my life history in front of them and the forms I had filled in were very searching – they just wanted to get you talking. When I was asked why I had chosen the WAAF I mumbled something about the Battle of Britain and they nodded to each other in approval. I was asked what experience I had in such a short time. I foolishly mentioned, rather flippantly, the shoe repairs and as a result I was told to rejoin my unit for a further three months, after which time I was to be reconsidered.

At the end of March 1942, I was called before the commission board again and this time I passed. In May I received posting instructions to report to the Officers' Cadet Training Unit (OCTU) at Grange-over-Sands. The WAAF officer school was in the Grand Hotel and after my previous few months I was quite bewildered to start with. Everything was completely different: the style of living was designed to get us used to life in an officers' mess and we appreciated the comparative comfort.

The course lasted four weeks. The lectures covered all aspects of service life and the responsibilities of an officer. We spent a lot of time studying King's Regulations and the manual of Air Force Law. There were examinations in all subjects, endless Drill Instruction and Physical Training. By the time we were commissioned we were expected to be able to take a parade and to know all the basic drill movements; we had very little spare time because all the evenings were taken up in learning notes from the day's lectures.

While we were at OCTU we were kitted out with our officer's uniform.

Several military tailors came to the school and displayed their goods in the hall. The initial outlay for the uniform was quite considerable and I was a little anxious about payment, as I had no bank account and did not want to ask any relatives to help.

But the majority of cadets were in the same position and we were allowed to pay as soon as our uniform grant came through. I thought the uniform was extremely smart. The barathea tunic and skirt was properly tailored and it was a relief to wear something that fitted exactly.

Posted to Headquarters Coastal Command at Northwood, I attended a lot of charges (under instruction). Mostly, airwomen were put on a charge for being absent without leave, absent from duty or for losing an item of equipment. These offences were dealt with quickly because in the majority of cases there were really no good excuses and the punishment was usually several days confined to camp and in the cases of lost equipment, a deduction of pay to make good a replacement.

Sometimes there would be a more serious offence and the accused would be asked by the officer, 'Will you accept my punishment or do you wish to be tried by a court martial?' There was always a sigh of relief when she said that she would accept the punishment. Certain offences had to be referred to higher authority and in this case a summary of evidence had to be taken. This was a statement by the accused, together with those of witnesses, and the case forwarded to group headquarters to be dealt with.

A WAAF band leads a parade through a town somewhere in England. Auxiliary forces often paraded through towns as part of war weapons weeks and other events to boost morale and raise funds for the war effort.

Sometimes a case was dealt with in the civil court and an officer had to go and say what she could in favour of the girl when her case came before the bench. I once went to court to speak about an airwoman's character; she had been charged by the civil authority with theft and some money had been found sewn inside her pillowcase. There had been a lot of petty pilfering in the unit and we had not been able to catch the culprit ourselves but the police had managed to track her down quite easily.

While at Northwood, I shared a room with a very retiring Irish girl called Maureen. Her work took her away a lot so I often had the room to myself. Much later, I read that she had been in training and was dropped by parachute into France with orders to contact the Maquis [French resistance]. She had to watch the movements of German troops and send and receive coded messages to London on her portable radio. She had certainly been involved in a most dangerous mission and I had never guessed. My own job was utterly boring by comparison but it was of course what I had been trained to do and I was still learning every day.

Trudy Murray (centre) with colleagues on signals at Chicksands, Bedfordshire, in 1944. All five women in this photograph are still in contact and three of them, including Trudy, married members of the Metropolitan Police. (T. Murray)

Trudy Murray was as a signals operator at Cranleigh in Surrey:

We worked with men – people from everywhere, who had come from their own countries to join the forces. We were not familiar with the word 'racism'.

A lot of the work was in code and teleprinted in blocks of five letters, so we didn't know what it was all about. Other work we typed from Morse tape and that came out as plain language so was more interesting. There were about fourteen teleprinter machines in the room and the same amount of people.

Our work was divided up into three shifts of 8 hours, 8 a.m. to 4 p.m., 4 p.m. to 12 a.m., and 12 a.m. to 8 a.m. We were only allowed to wear trousers on night duty. We had 36 hours off every eight days, two weeks holiday a year, never Christmas, as this was given to married men.

On a morning shift we would be up by 6, dress, tidy the hut, go to the cookhouse to line up for breakfast to be on duty for 8 to take over from the night shift. There were never slack times and we never cleared the work. It just kept coming in so one was never bored or hanging about.

During a shift we had one half-hour break for refreshment, which was usually soup or a doubtful sandwich. The camp cookhouse was nearly always open so we could get a meal there afterwards.

We all smoked like chimneys and ate too much NAAFI [the Navy, Army and Air Force Institute, which ran canteens for the forces] rubbish. We would cycle miles to go to a village dance and were not much welcomed by some of the village talent. The Americans entertained lavishly and were generous with sweets and cigarettes; some of the girls married them but most of my crowd were still single by the end of the war.

Demob was a big disappointment to a lot of us, it was an awful and wonderful war; I wouldn't have missed it for anything, some of the friends we made were forever.

CHAPTER 5

Women's Royal Naval Service

When the Women's Royal Naval Service (WRNS) was re-formed in 1939, it was originally intended as a part-time service. Those applying to be WRNS had to supply references and, given the limited number of places, many of that early intake were indeed relatives of serving or retired officers.

Initial duties were restricted to clerical, domestic and driving. Training started in 1939, with a WRNS ratings course following early the following year. The first officers' training course took place in late 1940. Many who joined up clearly did so in the hope of going to sea, but the director of the WRNS, Vera Laughton Mathews, dismissed such notions. In 1941, she said, 'At the beginning of the war, innumerable applicants caused amusement by emphasising their experience in boat work, sailing and navigation as qualifications for joining the WRNS. However, much as one might

Two views of a Wren bringing a boat into shore from 1942. (HMSO)

feel that these were women with very pleasant hobbies, one had continually to harden one's heart and say that these qualifications could not be made use of, but a knowledge of navigation is invaluable for shore appointments in which WRNS officers are, to a certain extent, replacing naval officers.'

However, the manpower crisis brought about a rapid expansion from 1941 onwards. Boat crews were established and began training. Manning small craft such as tugboats, they worked in harbours often in teams made up exclusively of women. Boat crews may not have gone into open waters but they had to be very skilful at handling craft. As one Wren later commented, 'For an eighteen-year-old it was very exciting and coming from boarding school too, I had never been independent before. We had to learn to handle a boat through all sorts of conditions, currents and huge seas in the Solent. We had to know all about the engine and how to maintain it.'

A government recruiting poster for the WRNS. (Crown Copyright)

The vast majority of Wrens served on shore, but as the range of duties expanded many were posted overseas. More than 100,000 women served in the WRNS during

---

WRNS Rank Structure

WRNS	RN Equivalent
Chief Commandant	Rear Admiral
Commandant	Commodore
Superintendent	Captain
Chief Officer	Commander
First Officer	Lieutenant-commander
Second Officer	Lieutenant
Third Officer	Sub-lieutenant

Debate continued throughout the war over whether women should bear arms. Meanwhile, a warrant officer was showing this Wren how to fire a rifle at an onshore naval establishment.

the war and by late 1944, the WRNS was at its peak, with nearly 75,000 personnel. They had a total of ninety rating and fifty officer levels. Wrens served all over the world and even formed the anti-aircraft guns on some naval air stations. The highest rank, chief commandant, was the female equivalent of a rear admiral.

Initially, women were not welcome at naval establishments. Mrs Laughton Mathews was as frank as the head of service could be in her remarks:

Perhaps the oldest and most conservative institution in the world and the most removed from feminine entanglements (at work), yet how splendidly the navy has withstood the shock of the introduction of women! Nothing could have been more generous than the way in which the navy has adapted the WRNS and has made it part of itself. It is not too much to say that this attitude of the navy has been the greatest factor in the success of the Sister Service.

True, in the early days there were naval officers who declared that they would fight against having WRNS to the last ditch, but they were few and far between. As one commanding officer said, 'I did not want WRNS but as I had to have them I made the best of them and I must say we have been very lucky in our WRNS!'

WOMEN'S ROYAL NAVAL SERVICE

WRNS UNIFORM

At first, the only item of uniform was a brassard with the letters 'WRNS', worn on the sleeve of civilian clothing. WRNS uniform had only been thought necessary in the First World War from January 1918, and even then, the basic uniform was quite unbecoming, especially when worn with the regulation heavy boots. WRNS officers, by contrast, had a uniform that was smarter than most, with more tailored lines.

WRNS ratings' first full uniform of the Second World War was a great improvement on the style of the first war. Made of rough serge, the double-breasted jacket had two flap pockets and horn buttons with the naval crown and fouled anchor. It was worn over a white shirt with detachable collar and black tie. A dark blue/black workshirt was the alternative for dirty work. The gored skirt, in the same blue serge, fell to just below the knee. Black stockings and four-eyelet, lace-up shoes completed the outfit. So smart was the uniform that after the war, the British airline BOAC bought up surplus WRNS clothing, including the tricorn hats, for the uniforms of their stewardesses.

Uniquely among the women's services, Wrens received an allowance of £3 for underwear. Given that they were issued with the universally despised dark-blue wool knickers and lisle stockings, this proved very useful. But the thick navy knickers had their uses, as

The range of adverts drawing on the services for inspiration and implicit endorsement was very wide but there were constant references to the servicewomen's sore feet.

Gwyneth Verdon-Roe (née Rogers) recalls: 'We used to turn the knickers upside down, sew across for shoulder seams, take out the gusset and make them into a jumper. We never wore them as knickers.'

Junior ranks wore a soft-crowned gabardine hat with a floppy brim but officers and senior ratings wore a tricorn hat with a light-blue wreath surrounding the fouled anchor device; male officers had a gold wreath. Others wore the traditional 'pork-pie' shaped sailor hat with, in the latter part of the war, just the letters 'HMS' in gold. It differed from the men's style in that it had a soft, unstiffened crown. Queen Elizabeth, later the Queen Mother – one of the great hat-wearers of the twentieth century, gave her personal approval to the WRNS hat after trying on several styles in front of a mirror at Buckingham Palace. This type of hat became fashionable with civilians throughout the war and remained so intermittently in peacetime. Other popular headgear included the blue headscarf and the beret.

Marion Dare (née Jones) recalls: 'One's hat band had always to be tied with a tiddly (very smart) bow and the sailor who tied mine put a sixpence in it to make sure it was really tiddly. I rather liked that sailor boy!'

WRNS working as cooks and stewards were given a work dress from 1940. Cooks, laundry maids and cleaners wore a short-sleeved, blue and white pinstriped knee-length button-through coverall trimmed with blue, and pockets at thigh level. Cooks also had a white apron and white chef's hat or headscarf. By

Scrubbing floors and other domestic cleaning duties were part of everyday life for Wrens. (HMSO)

1944, Wrens could opt for a short-sleeved navy cotton dress with a half-length button fastening, four plain plastic black buttons and two hip-level large patch pockets, and a buttoned-waisted belt.

Initially, Wrens shivered in gabardine raincoats, bought from civilian outfitters, but at the beginning of 1940 a heavy greatcoat, very similar again to that issued to naval men, was added to the uniform. The back of the coat had a pleat from shoulder to waist and a vent from below the waist to the bottom of the skirt, fastened together with buttons.

Soon outdoor workers were issued with other special clothing for cold weather. This included heavy woollen stockings and the ever-popular blue woollen knickers. Wrens also wore two-piece coverall suits, watch coats, duffel coats, oilskins and sea boots. This was usually 'Loan Clothing' because it was issued from a common store as needed and returned when the duties were over.

From 1941, Wrens served on small craft such as tugboats and harbour launches. This rapid and unexpected expansion of their duties meant that, for a while, they had to make do with men's uniforms, including the square-necked, white cotton

Three boats crew Wrens on a diesel boat in Plymouth, 1943. Left to right, Marjorie, June and Elizabeth. George is at the wheel. The Wrens spent nineteen months with this diesel vessel, living aboard every alternate twenty-four hours. (Author's Collection)

The same vessel taking a football party from HMS Ramilies *to a match.* (Author's Collection)

top, edged with navy blue, which was worn under their WRNS tunic. Women also wore the men's serge bell-bottomed trousers and white plimsolls with black soles. Female boats crews and boom defence Wrens could wear a white lanyard of their male counterparts' uniforms, under the collar of their tunics when in boating dress.

WRNS officers' uniforms, like those of the other two services, were based on those worn by their male officer equivalents. The dark-blue, double-breasted tunic in barathea, diagonal serge or doeskin had two slash pockets. A white handkerchief was often displayed on a small slash pocket on the left breast. The tunic had a double row of four gilt buttons, with the naval crown and fouled anchor motif with a rope-edging.

The WRNS, unlike the ATS and WAAF, had a tunic buttoning on the left – ladies – side. Officers left their top jacket button undone, following naval style known as Beatty tradition – a recent innovation named after the First World War hero who received the German naval surrender in 1918 and was First Sea Lord from 1919 to 1927.

WRNS officers' skirts were also better cut than the other services, with a double box pleat. For Angela Mack, one of the high points of the successful completion of officer training was choosing the tailors for a new uniform. In *Dancing on the Waves* she recalled: 'A friend wrote later to me, "Oh, the magic of the famous tailors coming down to Stoke Poges: Austin Reed, Gieves, Moss Bros . . . feeling that delicious doeskin cloth and weighing up which one to choose" . . . my friend was right about the doeskin; it was a minor miracle to have a properly cut uniform. . . . The literally crowning triumph was that hat. Whoever designed it was a genius. It suited nearly everyone I ever saw in it.'

All the WRNS rank and trade badges were embroidered in light blue, instead of the gold used on men's navy uniforms.

WRNS tropical uniforms were first issued in 1941, when a hand-picked group of twenty volunteer chief petty officer (CPO) Wrens and one second officer became the first to go abroad. The group was sent to Singapore so their uniform was extended to take into account the change of climate. This first version included a five-button (later reduced to four-button) short-sleeved shirtwaister-style dress. Large patch pockets at hip level and a belt fastened with hooks and eyes completed the look. In these early days, white cotton hat covers were issued to go over the first pattern (floppy) hat. The kit for the tropics also included a white-topped cap, white skirt, fastening on the left side with three buttons and

Drilling on the quarterdeck. (HMSO)

incorporating a pocket fastened by a single button. Buttons were in chromed metal or white plastic. Other items included a blue money belt, white stockings (often replaced by white ankle socks), and blanco for whitening the white canvas shoes and cap.

A tropical version of the new-style cap was introduced alongside the new general issue cap in 1942. It was identical to the new blue pattern except for the crown, which was white. A white pith helmet was essential for the climate and this would have a gilt metal badge and a blue fold in the puggaree (the thin scarf tied round to shield the neck). Later, the floppy officer's tropical hat was also issued to WRNS senior rates.

In late 1943, Angela Mack, now a WRNS signals officer, packed her tropical kit for a journey to the United States on board the RMS (Royal Merchant Ship) *Mauretania*.

Above: *A Wren signalling.* (Odhams) Left: *Semaphore signalling was still an essential part of communications at sea and ashore.* (HMSO)

We were to sail quite far south to avoid U-boat patrols and it began to get warmer . . . gradually the sea changed colour from all the shades of green to a deep, rich blue. Pieces of yellow seaweed floated by. We had reached the Gulf Stream. It was getting hotter by the hour and oppressive out of the breeze caused by the movement of ship. We used to rush to the dining room at meal times and beg for iced water. . . . The change into tropical kit improved everyone's appearance. The men wore shorts with long white socks and white shoes and had white covers to their caps. They told us that when we docked in New York, they would have to change back into long trousers if they went ashore as shorts were not approved wear in the USA.

The *Mauretania* began its journey back to Liverpool, packed with American servicemen and servicewomen. Angela Mack continues:

On the next night out, some time after dinner, I decoded the message: 'To the Captain, RMS *Mauretania* . . . U-boat in your vicinity 15N by 42W.'

This had to be got up to the bridge fast. I double-checked the degrees, locked the cipher office and went in search of the captain. To get to the bridge, in complete darkness, one had to climb through a series of blacked-out compartments, made light-tight, so to speak, by heavy black curtains. Between the last two curtains, I had to feel my way up the companion way, like a blind man. Suddenly I was aware of the fresh air and that I was standing on the bridge, the holy of holies, and that there were figures standing about, peering through the darkness.

I asked for the Captain and informed him that I had an urgent signal for him. He did not, as I expected, step back through the black-out curtains to take the signal from me but instead asked me what it said. With a horrified intake of breath – supposing I got the degrees wrong? – I repeated it to him. This would not seem to be an achievement, but I have never been able to remember figures. Luckily Mercury, the undoubted god of naval communications, stood by my elbow.

The Captain immediately told me to get a life jacket and gave the order for the ship's company to carry them. (Everyone except ship's crew wore life jackets all the time.)

It was electrifying. There was a calm and orderly stir throughout the ship as everyone took up their action stations. In the Asdic room [the room in which the submarine detection equipment was kept], the tension was like a taut wire

A well-worn white ensign is hoisted as a WRNS officer comes aboard. (HMSO)

Meteorological Wrens calculate and plot the speed and direction of the wind. (HMSO)

and no one spoke at all. I went back to the cipher office wondering if we should get another signal.

I stared at the tightly fastened porthole and listened to the steady comforting noise of the ship's engine. We were really moving, the forward thrust through the water had greatly increased. One sensed the concentration of everyone's thoughts on board. If being condemned to death concentrates the mind wonderfully, I thought, then so does the picture of the two of us, the U-boat and the *Mauretania*, nearing each other in the otherwise lonely north Atlantic. It was rather too easy to picture the U-boat captain, peering at us through his periscope and ordering 'Actung, achtung, torpedoes ready. . . .'. I thought that if we had to jump overboard I must remember to unlace and kick off my shoes. The despised, rather dirty white life jacket might be useful. After all, we were all, passengers and crew, literally in the same boat now.

We did not know how the position of the U-boat had been discovered and the warning sent. It is possible that the U-boat captain was unaware that we were in the vicinity and had surfaced to send a message which enabled his location to be pin-pointed. Now we know that the warning came to us via the secret station at Bletchley, where the German codes were broken. In those days, we knew nothing whatever about Ultra. It made exciting reading after the war and I felt personally grateful to the skill and vigilance of many, including my future sister-in-law.

As allied troops from America and other countries flooded into Britain in preparation for the invasion of Europe, Wrens were being recruited and sent to the south coast of England. Marion Dare was nineteen when she decided to join the WRNS in 1942.

After two weeks, I was called for an interview with Madame Coode-Bate, the senior WRNS officer in the Bristol Channel area (HMS *Lucifer*).

At this time, the first preparations were being made for the invasion of Europe and looking back and remembering the subjects that were raised at that interview, I now realise that I was being vetted not only for qualifications but also for security for the job that was to be my life for the next four years.

I was told to report to Madam Coode-Bate, at the naval headquarters in Mountstewart Square in Cardiff. Before I even had time to get my uniform I was given an office and as I was settling in, the 'phone rang and I answered it.

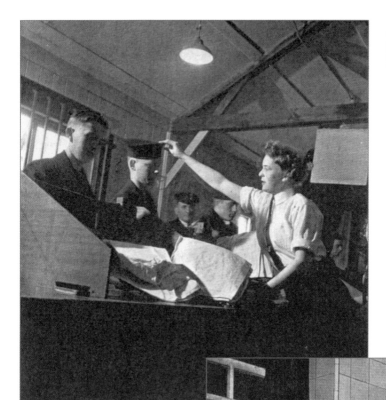

A supply assistant kitting out new recruits to the Royal Navy. (HMSO)

Dinner for hundreds was an everyday order for these Wren cooks at an onshore naval establishment. (HMSO)

A voice asked, 'Hello, is your name Marion? If so, would you come in and see me?' Not knowing where to go, I asked another Wren and she told me which office to go to. I knocked on the door and went into a large office in which was sitting Admiral Sir Rudolph Burmester, Admiral Bristol Channel Area, my new boss. I was to be his personal secretary.

I dealt only with the admiral and the base captain. Because the work I was doing was not just 'Top Secret' but 'Too Secret', I could not go to the canteen for a cup of tea, but had it brought in to me. The windows of my office were whitewashed, I had to burn my carbon papers, and my typewriter was locked away when it was not in use.

I took all the minutes of the meetings of the senior officers of the services planning Operation Neptune and Operation Turnabout in the Bristol area. 'Neptune' was the code name for the D-Day landings, 'Turnabout' was bringing the men, ships and so on back. I sat at my little table in the admiral's office and recorded everything said by the admiral, the district shipyard controller, the heads of the army and the air force, and any other experts brought to the conferences, numbering them for identification purposes – '2 said . . .', '4 said . . .', and so on.

Back in my own office, I would make a fair copy, which would be amended if necessary by the admiral. Then I had to prepare five copies, the sheets of each copy tied together through a hole at the top left hand corner with green ribbon sealed with wax and then knotted, and mark each copy, 'Too Secret'.

Three copies were distributed by the WRNS motorcyle dispatch rider to the heads of the army, air force and the area shipyard controller; the admiral had one and the spare copy was locked up with my type-

Wren motorcyclists leave the Admiralty in London with dispatches. (Odhams)

Learning their trade: Wrens in training as wireless telegraphy operators. It was Wrens who were later drafted into Bletchley Park where they took down messages for the Enigma code-breakers. (Odhams)

writer and the carbon papers were burned. It was all very exciting indeed but I was not allowed to socialise with the other WRNS or sailors, knowing as I did all the plans and even the target date for the invasion.

After the landings took place and were successful, I landed in the sick bay for a week under twilight sleep medication.

Admiral Sir Rudolph Burmester then left to become, I believe, governor of Tasmania, and I became secretary to Admiral Sir Hugh Binney, who replaced him, and so it all went on – except that I was now less restricted in my contacts.

Among other postings, Moira Shepherd worked on communications at Combined Forces HQ, Dover Command, based in Dover Castle. 'In 1944 I viewed D-Day, a sight never to be forgotten with all the aircraft above and the fleet in the channel.'

When Gwyneth Verdon-Roe (née Rogers) joined the WRNS in 1943, her father and her brother Keith were already in the Royal Navy. After training in Scotland, she was posted as a plotter; she often recorded their ships as they came into

Liverpool after accompanying merchant ships across the Atlantic. In letters home – censor permitting – she kept her mother up to date with their progress:

Western Approaches, Liverpool, Christmas 1943

On night duty once more. Won't it be super if Daddy can get home for Christmas? Looking at the plot now I can see six convoys almost in. I wonder? I could have jumped over the moon when I heard Daddy is home. Marvellous – he is home for Christmas which solves a lot of problems. To think I plotted him in without realising. We had six convoys arriving in the past few days, all rushing home for Christmas, never been so hectic all night on the go, but well worth it when I think of all the men like Daddy who will be home for the holiday. Out of six convoys it is impossible to guess which one Pop was on, therefore I can't tell where he has been sent. The convoys split up outside the Mersey so he could have gone to Clyde, Belfast, or Barrow, but my guess is the Clyde where most of the American convoys go.

When I came in last night the officer had been looking everywhere for me as she was sorry I had missed my Christmas dinner and had saved it for me. So I had my third helping of turkey and Christmas pudding. The first was from the kind ladies of the WVS, eaten when I was on night duty at 1 a.m., the

Learning the various signals from a Royal Navy signals officer. (HMSO)

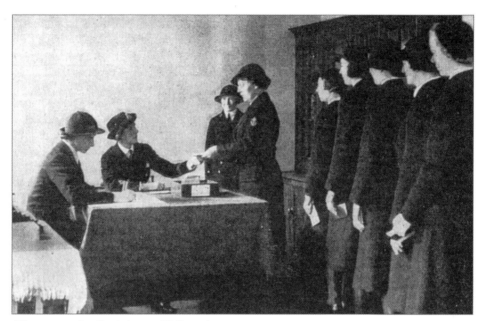

Wrens mustering for their pay. (Odhams)

second I had at lunchtime at the Naval Club – so now my tummy feels like a barrage balloon. I am off to hear a rendering of the Messiah.

Thank you for the money I received this morning but is £3 and NO COUPONS all you could get for my overcoat? It was a good coat so I'm not very happy about it but the money will come in useful. Work has been heavy this week with four plotters off sick, on top of which we have been plotting enemy aircraft – terrifically exciting but more than hectic and a bit much to cope with – I will need my weekend off if I can get it. . . . Had a letter from Doreen. Her boyfriend has definitely been killed – she is so miserable. Isn't it dreadful – ninety-six bombers missing yesterday again.

In one letter, she recounted a startlingly daring theft:

My last but one duty on nights. . . . I had a most exciting day today – I went to bed at 9 a.m. after a long night but with six girls trailing in and out of the cabin I could not sleep. At noon Pam came in and saw I was wide awake and suggested we went to the pantomime matinée to cheer ourselves up. So we dressed, powdered our noses and off we went on the train.

Passing through the docks, we saw ORANGES. Piles of them. So we nipped off the train, coolly walked past the guards on the dock gates and picked as many oranges as we could carry of the ones not rotting on the ground and a nice policeman gave us a newspaper to wrap them in. Staggering under our load we hitched a lift in a lorry full of workmen and they gave us a toolbag in which to carry our spoils. We dropped the oranges off at the Liver building and as it was obviously our lucky day, walked back to the docks again walking past the guards. We saw amazing ships – one full of Americans packed like sardines and another with RAF chaps disembarking. We knew many of the ships from plotting them and Pam saw one that had a friend aboard so we went to see if he was there and he was. They gave us a terrific welcome, fed us on scones and butter and showed us round the destroyer and especially showed us how they plotted their course and how the 'ping' anti-submarine radar worked. They insisted on us staying to dinner which was great fun with officers to amuse us. . . . It was a marvellous day.

By March 1944, Gwyneth was in Devon, at the Dartford Naval College:

Clifton Cottage
Devon, glorious Devon! The weather is perfect. The flowers are blooming and the air feels wonderfully fresh and clean. The Operations Room is smaller than the Western Approaches and much more casual and friendly, with windows looking out over the river.

The best news is that we are on four watches, child's play – a rest cure. Collected our tin helmets and were then taken to our quarters, a cottage on a hill overlooking the river on one side and the sweetest garden on the other. It is too good to be true – I have to keep pinching myself. There are three other girls in our cabin – all boat crew. We will have so much time off in comparison with the plotters in Liverpool, our hearts bleed for them. . . . When I look back, I think that the plotters are meant to be superhuman in Liverpool and really too much is asked of them. . . . Keith says he wants a Mars bar for his birthday. He is hopeless. I don't know what to give him.

The WRNS had the usual Sunday hop last night. Great fun but it is confusing dancing with Englishmen and then with Americans, their dancing is so completely different.

20 April – a postcard
In case you saw Goebbels' remarks in the newspaper about Dartmouth being flames from buzz bombs, I thought I had better set any fears at rest by telling you I have seen nothing more harmful than a seagull flying around.

A pilot with the Fleet Air Arm is given permission to take off by a leading WRNS visual signaller with a 10-in projector. (HMSO)

A WRNS drum and bugle band on board HMS Ganges. (HMSO)

Wrens in the airing room of a Fleet Air Arm station packing parachutes. (Odhams)

I read your letter at breakfast and am writing straight away to put your mind at rest. . . . It is all a nonsense and we haven't had a siren or a buzz bomb for ages.

By the end of the month, D-Day preparations still allowed for one last dance – under escort for security purposes.

29 May 1944

We are not allowed to go out at all now and even the laundry is restricted. There is a dance at the college tonight and we will be escorted there to dance to Artie Shaw's band. . . . Tomorrow I have my medical before going to Plymouth on Wednesday for the overseas board, staying overnight so I can visit the operations room. I am looking forward to the break. . . . The privilege to wear civvies has been withdrawn because two girls wore them to go aboard an American ship. Damn!

6 June, 3.30 hours

I know there was no mail and you must have been worried. I have written but now the invasion has started perhaps the post will arrive. We have to be so careful – not much that I can tell you that will pass the Censor but I think it's all right to say that for the past week, I have been completely cut off, escorted to and from duty via special routes and not allowed out otherwise even to other WRNS quarters. Just had to work and sit around. Couldn't write letters, even if I could there was nothing I could say, so I slept, read, and got my mending, washing and ironing up to date. We were not allowed to go into shops and I was short of soap.

A Wren at work on a teleprinter in this scene from the Ministry of Information film W.R.N.S. (HMSO)

We couldn't 'phone, send telegrams or speak to anyone, either service or civilian. Now it is all over and we can be proud. We worked long hard hours and it was worth it. We had to be so secretive that I can't get used to mentioning the word 'invasion' out loud and felt like hushing the BBC newsreader.

9 June
It is difficult to tell you anything discreetly. I am looking after Daddy's ship but he is in a confusion of other ships. I watched all the ships go by on D-Day from the top of the hill and saw Keith pass in the distance. It was a very impressive sight indeed – like the Armada. We can hear the guns of the bombardment on the French coast from here.

Soon after D-Day, like many women in the forces, Gwyneth's work had earned her promotion.

24 September
I am a LEADING WREN! The ceremony was a hoot – very serious and official. The Petty Officer put on her glasses and the hat. I marched into the room and saluted, the Petty Officer said something, the First Officer said something and the Commanding Officer congratulated me. I should get my full pay of £3 5s soon. I'm in the money!

By the time the war ended, Gwyneth had been posted to Immingham in Lincolnshire:

2 May 1945
I am sitting in a huddle over the gas fire, listening to the news. What an anticlimax that there are no real peace moves after all. I wonder if Hitler is really dead? It is hard to believe. Every watch I wonder how near it is to the last one and when the war will end.

In her final letter home during the war, Gwyneth wrote: 'Lots of ships are going over to the Hook of Holland to take part in a thanksgiving service and victory march. I wish they would take the WRNS, we are good at marching out of step.'
    Angela Mack viewed demobilisation with mixed feelings:

Now we had to press on with the task of learning a trade and earning our living. . . . The Wrens wisely and generously had devised the Vocational Training

Scheme. . . . I might have tried for a university place but it never occurred to me to have a go. I did what most people seemed to be doing and took a secretarial course, often getting into trouble for being late back after lunch. There were too many delightful people on leave or just demobbed and how could one hurry back to pothooks, if lunch at Claridges or the Savoy was offered? We were all indulging in a postwar spree of spending our demob pay in a splendid last extravagance, despite the careful advice, before getting down to 'real' life once more.

Women in the forces, Angela Mack says,

. . . did their bit to change the pre-war ideas that had got deep frozen in the male mind. It was not only that they had learnt to take orders, they had also been trained to use their initiative.

Towards the end of 1945, a naval captain of some renown begged a group of us, when the war was over, to go back to wearing evening dress to the opera and to the theatre. He deplored the casual wearing of uniform and day clothes which, in his opinion, spoilt what should be an 'occasion'. 'All you young women should make a determined effort to get back to the days of elegance,' he said. It seemed a lovely idea. What more splendid aim than to be truly feminine again. And yet . . . I wondered if there was not more between the lines of this request; I had a suspicion he was also implying that we should take up the role of dear, obedient woman-at-home once more. I feared that this vision of pre-war womanhood, charming as it might be, did rather place us like chess pieces on a centuries-old board, where our moves were too clearly defined. I had a suspicion that after serving in His Majesty's Forces, some of us had other ideas.

In time our greatcoats, and jackets, with their markings removed, were sent to Oxfam but for a long time I and, I suspect, others, hid our tricorns away. I was fiercely fond of mine: it represented at least one achievement, just in case I didn't get any others.

CHAPTER 6

Military Nursing Services

Nursing services, civilian and military, were in a chaotic state long before the outbreak of war in 1939. Civilian nursing services were so understrength that the government abolished the minimal entry qualification to encourage recruitment, and set up a Committee of Inquiry, chaired by the Earl of Athlone, to report on the problems. National pay scales, higher wages, shorter hours and subsidies to teaching hospitals to support nurse training were all recommended in the Athlone interim report, published in 1939.

The report looked at the low levels of recruitment to nursing. It found that many potential recruits were dissuaded by the petty discipline which was a feature of a service based on an essentially military structure. Many people held the view that nursing was an extension of mothering, rather than the result of three years of training, which also rankled with qualified nurses. This view was certainly current in the military nursing services as well, but with higher pay, officer status and an empathy with the structure, traditions and genealogy of the regular army, military nurses were the elite.

Military nursing was the only female service to continue after the end of the First World War but its customs dated back to the earliest days of the nursing service founded by Florence Nightingale during the Crimean War of 1853–6. From that time, military nurses had nominal officer status. More significantly in the class-based British society, military nurses were drawn from the families of officers, and recruitment was on the basis that military nurses were born and not made. Royal patronage, which had an especially high profile during the First World War, was another important factor.

Queen Alexandra's Imperial Military Nursing Service (QAIMNS) provided nursing services to the army in clearing stations, field hospitals and in military bases. The service was established in 1902. At the outbreak of the Second World War, QAIMNS had only 700 members but was boosted by those on the reserve list and by the mobilisation of the Territorial Army

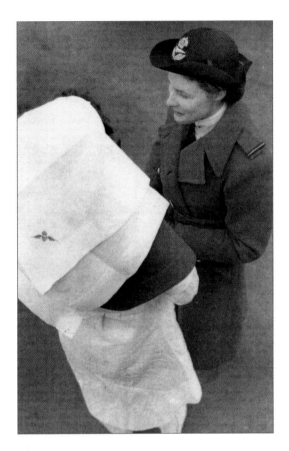

Two members of Princess Mary's Royal Air Force Nursing Service. Popularly referred to as PMs, those serving in this branch of military nursing had a hat similar to the tricorn style worn by WRNS officers and senior ratings, but with a fourth corner at the back. Also clearly visible in this picture is the emblem of the PMRAFNS, embroidered on the point at the back of the veil. (Imperial War Museum)

Nursing Services (TANS), not to mention the influx of the Voluntary Aid Detachments (VADs).

As the Second World War broke out, the royal connections were still very much in evidence: Queen Mary was president of Queen Alexandra's Royal Naval Nursing Service (QARNNS) and head of Queen Alexandra's Imperial Military Nursing Service. The RAF Nursing Service, originally formed in 1918 and renamed Princess Mary's Royal Air Force Nursing Service (PMRAFNS) in 1923, was headed by the Princess Royal at the time of the outbreak of the Second World War.

UNIFORMS AND RANKS IN MILITARY NURSING SERVICES

Nurses' uniforms altered drastically, reflecting their changing role. The traditional dresses and starched white aprons were totally impractical for nursing at the front line, especially in tropical locations.

Army Nursing Structure
Nurses had nominal officer status from 1904, and in 1941 were granted the King's Commission and rank badges in the following ranks:

QAIMNS	Army Equivalent
Matron-in-Chief	Brigadier
Chief Principal Matron	Colonel
Principal Matron	Lieutenant-Colonel
Matron	Major
Senior Sister	Captain
Sister	Lieutenant

Queen Alexandra had chosen service colours of grey and scarlet when she had founded the service in 1902. The dress for daily work (ward dress) was, therefore, grey and was worn with a short red cape (tippet). One of the two breast pockets was designed to hold a thermometer or pen. Long sleeves were fastened by two buttons at the cuff. The collar was detachable and in starched white cotton. The badge of the service was embroidered on the back of the veil: the QAIMNS had a cloth rose; the TANS had a silver 'T' on each front point of their tippets. On the silver badge of the QAIMNS the full title was spelled out with the motto *Sub*

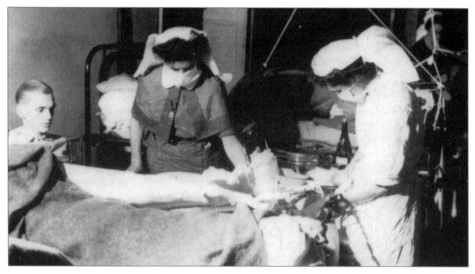

A member of QUAIMNS (centre) in a European hospital. (Imperial War Museum)

As nurses were needed at the battle front, their uniforms became more like those worn by male soldiers. These nurses were setting up a field hospital when General Montgomery (centre) paid a visit. (Imperial War Museum)

Cruce Candida (Under the Sign of the White Cross). In the centre was the Cross of Danebourg and the initial letter 'A' for Alexandra, and the whole was surmounted by the king's crown. QAIMNS (Reserve) members wore a silver badge with the title of the service spelled out in full in a circle (garter) round the letter 'R'. An embroidered shoulder badge, bearing the letters 'Q.A.I.M.N.S.' in white on a maroon background was introduced late in the war but is rarely seen.

A more economical printed version was also made. Shoulder boards denoting rank were also worn on the tippet.

Nurses also wore starched white aprons with bib fronts that tied at the back – totally unsuitable in field hospitals. In fact, anything white, especially items had to be starched, caused particular problems. This was especially true for nurses in hot climates where, as they often reported, even if the water supply was reliable, it was not necessarily clean enough for washing and starching white clothing.

So from 1942, while serving in the field, nursing sisters wore battledress blouse and trousers – male or ATS, depending on availability. Sometimes, the service cap would be worn with the badge of a particular service to indicate that its wearer was a nurse, and as officers, nurses wore rank insignia epaulettes.

Materials for nursing uniforms became especially difficult to find as shortages worsened, so from January 1944 nurses wore the same khaki uniform as ATS officers. From this point, nurses were distinguishable by the double lanyards in scarlet and grey, reminiscent of the old uniform colours. The individual nursing services were denoted by cap and collar badges.

Other gear for tropical climes included anti-mosquito uniforms, worn where the risk of malaria was so great that regardless of the heat, everyone had to be covered from head to foot in a heavy cotton drill uniform, spats, netting hood worn over the bush hat and special gloves. Equally essential was an individual DDT spray (insecticide).

Field dress was revised and a more practical version introduced in 1944. The field force dress was in traditional grey and had large, detachable patch pockets at hip level, larger breast pockets, detachable sleeves and a buckled belt of matching grey fabric. It was fastened at the front with concealed plastic buttons. The sleeves were each secured with four buttons, and the detachable white starched collar was replaced with an integral soft grey version in the same material as the rest of the dress. Detachable epaulettes in service colours denoted rank. For those serving in the field, headgear was sometimes the service issue cap, but steel helmets were, of necessity, just as common.

THE TERRITORIAL ARMY NURSING SERVICE

The Territorial Army Nursing Service badge was in white metal and silver. It spelled out the full name of the service and carried the TANS motto, *Fortitudo Mea Deus* (God is my Strength). In the centre was the cypher of Queen Alexandra and this was surmounted by the king's crown.

NAVAL NURSES

Queen Alexandra's Royal Naval Nursing Service

Naval Nursing Structure	
QARNNS	**WRNS**
Matron-in-Chief	Commandant
Principal Matron	Superintendent
Matron	Chief Officer
Superintending Sister	First Officer
Senior Nursing Sister	Second Officer
Nursing Sister	Third Officer

The QARNNS was the smallest of the three military nursing services. Before 1939, it had only 200 nursing sisters and a supplementary reserve of civilian sisters who were called up at the outbreak of war. Even at its peak, it numbered little more than 7,000 members.

Naval nursing sisters wore a dark-blue working dress on the wards with full-length button fastening, a white starched apron and detachable collar and cuffs. Formal wear meant the dark-blue tippet with narrow red trim and waist belt. The wearer's rank was displayed in the lower right front corner of the tippet. The basic badge had a king's crown, an anchor entwined with Queen Alexandra's cypher, and red cross. Wartime economies dictated that the gold and silver wire used in the badges was later replaced by non-metallic thread. Senior nursing staff tippets had a broad red trim. The textured silk fabric waist belt had a large metal buckle in white metal depicting a crown and anchor with laurel wreath. Naval nursing sisters also wore a white veil-type head covering, fastened bearing an embroidered royal blue insignia. QARNNS officers could wear the same uniform as WRNS officers when not in ward dress but unlike WRNS officers, their rank insignia was worn on the epaulettes rather than the cuff rings. The cap badge was a king's crown surmounting the anchor entwined with the cipher of Queen Alexandra, and the cipher and anchor were enclosed by a narrow border. In the tropics, they wore a lightweight white cotton dress, white tippet with red trim, white belt and hat similar in style to that worn by the WRNS officers.

During an official visit to the naval base at Rosyth, the Duchess of Kent, Commandant of the WRNS, talks to a reserve sister wearing the ward dress uniform of Queen Alexandra's Royal Naval Nursing Service. (Imperial War Museum)

AIR FORCE NURSES

Princess Mary's Royal Air Force Nursing Service

Air Force Nursing Structure

PMRAFNS	RAF
Matron-in-Chief	Air Commodore
Principal Matron	Wing Commander
Matron	Squadron Leader
Senior Sister	Flight Lieutenant
Sister	Flying Officer
Staff Nurse (up to I April 1941)	Pilot Officer

Four PMRAFNS sisters in a 1943 publicity photograph. The sister on the left wears the black 'four-cornered' hat; the other three the storm cap. (Imperial War Museum)

The Royal Air Force Nursing Service was formed almost as soon as the Royal Air Force itself, in June 1918. Five years later it became Princess Mary's Royal Air Force Nursing Service.

The PMRAFNS service dress was in blue-grey barathea with a skirt falling to mid-calf (long for the time) and a Norfolk-style jacket, which was distinctive for the two panel pleats that ran the full length of the front and back. The jacket had three brass or gilt buttons and a cloth full belt fastened at the front with two more buttons. The skirt had two smaller pleat panels on the front only. Black shoes and stockings completed the outfit. In winter, service dress was a blue-grey barathea coat-style dress with long sleeves, half-length front closure and twelve small gilt buttons. It was worn with a matching tippet with a gilt caduceus in each front corner. Uniquely in the RAF, PMRAFNS wore white shirts with their black ties, rather than the traditional blue. Official summer dress included two styles of hat: the black 'four-cornered' version and the blue-grey storm cap. On the ward, the PMs wore a white dress fastened with fourteen buttons down to hip level, with short sleeves, a half front belt and head veil. They wore the caduceus emblem on their collar points.

After 1941, single rank stripes remained, denoting different 'appointments' – light blue on maroon for matrons and senior sisters, light on dark blue for sisters until 1943. From that time they wore the light blue and black lace rank insignia of the RAF and WAAF at the cuffs, while retaining the nursing title equivalents. A RAF grey-blue tippet with the caduceus emblem on each point was worn with this uniform too. In the field, the ward dress was replaced with the serge service skirt and WAAF battledress blouse. Epaulettes were added to display rank lace.

Despite their elite status, or because of the way in which it was maintained, military nursing services were, if anything, even more understrength than the civilian equivalent at the start of the war, and the shortages worsened as time passed. Stringent selection procedures dominated recruitment. Those entering military nursing services had to do their initial training in civilian hospitals. One argument put forward for maintaining the harsh and petty discipline that so dissuaded would-be recruits to nursing was that it prepared those trainee civilian nurses who would eventually work under military discipline.

Another development that influenced the military nursing services was rapid progress and expansion of the newly created ATS. Dame Katherine Jones was the matron-in-chief and her primary concern was that in the military, registered nurses should be fully commissioned officers. This meant nurses had to be regarded as soldiers first. She argued that the ATS established itself in this way and the result was that everyone recognised an officer in the ATS as an army officer first and foremost. Her aim was to achieve the same for the military nursing service and in doing so, the hope was that the elevated status would reflect positively on the civilian equivalent.

A patient is loaded onto an ambulance aircraft by orderlies of the PMRAFNS. (Imperial War Museum)

Many of the lessons that could have been learned from the Spanish Civil War had to re-learned during the Second World War. But one important development that had been acknowledged was the need to treat the wounded on the battlefield. This was known as the Trueta system after the Spanish surgeon who identified and developed the approach. The implications were that nurses needed to be stationed near to the front line, a strategic decision that meant many military nurses worked in the areas of greatest danger during the war.

Nurses now had to take on the training necessary for life at the front. Many had to undergo intensive fitness programmes and wear battledress. The military was still convinced that nurses were invaluable for boosting the morale of fighting troops, but little else. In this respect there was little variation in the attitudes towards trained nurses and voluntary support services such as the VADs and the Civil Nursing Reserve.

The Voluntary Aid Detachment had been formed in 1910 at the instigation of the Army Council. VADs, as they were known, were trained by the British Red Cross and the Order of St John and St Andrew's Ambulance Association. Duties were wide-ranging, especially as the shortages in nursing staff worsened. VADs might do anything from cooking, changing beds and driving ambulances to taking care of injured military personnel in transit and running dressing stations and emergency hospitals. As in the First World War, they were posted overseas as well as at home. The vast majority of VADs were stationed with the army but a few were with the navy. With the customary inter-service rivalry between the various branches of the military, the Royal Air Force created its own nursing auxiliary, independent of the VADs.

The Athlone interim report in 1939 could do nothing to stop the flow of nurses from civilian services into military nursing at the start of the war. Military nursing could offer better conditions, pay and status than the civilian equivalent.

Meanwhile, Dame Katherine Jones continued to push for commissioned officer status for all military nurses and within two years, in 1941, this was given to all state registered nurses in the armed forces. In that year, over 80,000 registered nurses were available for work, of whom 9,000 were with military services and 24,000 in the civilian sector. The vast majority of the remainder had therefore opted out of nursing altogether.

Further developments to encourage recruitment into, particularly, civilian nursing continued. However, by 1943, the government was forced to restrict the numbers of trained nurses in key specialities from going into the armed forces. Given that the problem was of an overall shortage which simply affected civilian

Members of Queen Alexandra's Imperial Military Nursing Service unpacking supplies at No. 79 General Hospital at Bayeux, France. (Imperial War Museum)

nursing to a greater degree than the military service, it was inevitable that the forces, too, were desperately short of nurses.

However, military nurses were very much in evidence from the beginning of the war. They accompanied the British Expeditionary Force across to France. Colonel Margaret Kneebone recalled the withdrawal of the BEF from France in spring 1940:

It was crowded and it was the first time I had seen battle exhaustion. It was a pathetic sight. Their faces were blue and they were just too tired to move. . . . We got the order to take no more patients. So I went to my Red Cross Store and I got enormous quantities of supplies: mittens, socks, gloves and everything else. I gathered them up and thought 'the Germans shan't have these'. And I went and gave them all to the orderlies and anybody else who wanted them. . . . Just about midday, while I was in the quartermaster's stores a company officer, a very smart territorial, came to the door and saluted me saying, 'Madam the order has come, immediate movement, get into the ambulances. . . . You cannot go to the billet to collect your things.' Four of my sisters were down at the billet having lunch. Not one of them said a word. I brought them up on laws – not to question why, yours but to do or die!

Back on British soil, Colonel Kneebone continues:

> For days and nights, all kinds of ships plied to and fro across the Channel under the fierce onslaught of the enemy's bombers. As each ship came in, the army doctors at the port would shout out to the captain on the bridge to ask for the number of wounded. In a few minutes the ambulances and stretchers would be alongside to bring them off and take them to the waiting hospital trains. . . . The organisation in the port was excellent. The ships were unloaded at an astonishing speed and no sooner were they empty than they were disappearing though the harbour entrance back to France to fetch more men home.

The decision to move nurses to the front line changed everything about the way they worked, and soon they were learning about the vagaries of working in the heat of North Africa. One nurse recalled that although the flies and dust of Egypt were the worst aspects of the country, the flies actually helped with the healing process. 'As you were dressing the patients, of course the flies came round in swarms, but they had been using the Trueta treatment of cleaning them up on the battlefield, and although when you got them back and came to dress them [the wounds] were often crawling with maggots, which the patients used to think was dreadful, you got used to it. You would say to them "don't worry, tomorrow it will be all right", and of course it was just nature's way of healing. Those wounds healed beautifully.'

At the start of the war, matron-in-chief Katherine Jones had resisted the army's preference for nurses to be ministering angels. Her view was that they should be full of masculine efficiency and, as Penny Starns put it in *Nurses at War*, 'The change of image from angel to battleaxe was just another step on the road to commissioned officer status and full military recognition of the worth of registered nurses. As Dame Katherine herself acknowledged, "If I survive at all in nursing history, I shall doubtless survive as the militarising Matron-in-Chief. I am glad that should be so."'

In 1941, Dame Katherine achieved her goal of full commissioned officer status for military registered nurses. It was assumed by the nursing press and the profession that one of the benefits would be protection for nurses if they were captured. As subsequent experiences, especially in the Far East, showed, this was a false hope. Many thousands of nurses, military and civilian, were raped, starved, killed and otherwise brutalised as the Japanese swept into Malaya, Hong Kong, the Philippines and Singapore.

British nurses generally took their new status quite seriously – unlike their equivalents in other allied forces. Jean Crameri, an Australian nursing sister recorded her matron's attitude: 'Matron thought we would have some practice at Eyes Right. So she placed a nurse as governor and we all turned Eyes Right. Then instead of Eyes Front Matron sang out Eyes Left – everyone roared out laughing.'

As the war progressed, so the medical conditions facing military nurses changed. Nurse Johnston was a sister with the QA Reserves, and was among those tending thousands of Polish prisoners of war:

Practically every disease in medical knowledge could be found among them and particularly deficiency diseases, dysentery, typhus and malaria. . . . My first reaction was to collect materials and spend half an hour cleaning the mouth of a man who was obviously nearing the end of his life but having much difficulty breathing his last. An hour later a sepoy told me he was dead. That incident snapped something in me; it was clear what must, in broad outline, be done. The individual must be sacrificed; for one trained person to cope with 200 or so in this condition it was obviously impossible to nurse even a fraction as they should be nursed until the place was properly organised.

In 1943, the Nurses Act attempted to rectify the shortages in civilian nursing. In a rather extraordinary act of wishful thinking, the government decided that new drug therapies, especially penicillin, would reduce the demand for military nurses. Other developments, such as treating facial injuries in special units near to the front line, caused a huge reduction in mortality rates, but the mobile units that were so important to their success needed nurses as well as doctors.

After D-Day, military nurses were inevitably essential as allied forces fought across Europe, liberating occupied countries and more specifically, those people held in concentration camps. Typhus was rife – Josef Kramer, the commandant of Belsen, negotiated a surrender to the British because he feared the typhus epidemic would spread through Germany if the camp's inmates escaped.

The liberation of the concentration camps brought nurses face to face with a profession corrupted by Nazism. In Hitler's Germany, nurses before and during the war had routinely selected patients in their care for lethal injections and had assisted in experiments on Jews, Slavs, gypsies, disabled people and others deemed *Untermensch* (Subhuman). When Belsen and other camps were liberated, the German nurses were forced to tend to the camp victims.

Back in Britain, the *British Journal of Nursing* called for the death penalty for those nurses guilty of war crimes. Once the countries in the Far East had been liberated, military nurses testified to their own brutal treatment as prisoners of the Japanese.

As the war ended, nurses were in even greater demand as Europe struggled to recover from the devastation. Many, such as Nurse Kitchner, found life after demobilisation dull by comparison. Shortly after demob, she wrote, 'I miss the moves of the army as I travelled quite a long way – Norway . . . Palestine and Egypt, France and Belgium. . . . I went over to France five weeks after D-Day and wallowed in mud and rain (we were in a tented hospital) for weeks before we moved into Belgium, a most interesting two-day journey in lorries. My posting to Germany came at the same time as my release and I was awfully sorry not to go.'

Military nurses were demobilised as their services were put on a peacetime footing. After the war, the QAIMNS were renamed Queen Alexandra's Royal Army Nursing Corps. The other military nursing services also changed their names in similar fashion.

Military nurses' salary scales were adjusted upwards first, to achieve parity with other women officers and then once again to recognise that military nurses, by definition, had to have a professional qualification, while other officers did not.

Even though the services were reduced drastically to peacetime levels, vacancies inevitably occurred. In 1946, the *British Journal of Nursing* reported that QAIMNS was to be reduced to 624 members from a wartime peak of 12,000. In the same article, the *BJN* reported that nearly 60 nurses were competing for 11 vacancies in QARNS.

Civilian nursing, despite measures to encourage recruitment, still could not offer the status and pay of military nursing. Shortages of civilian nurses at one point threatened the future of the fledgling National Health Service. It is an issue that still affects civilian nursing services today.

CHAPTER 7

Final Days

When the war was over, many women in the auxiliary forces, like those who had taken on civilian jobs, went back home, married and had families. The clear understanding all along was that women had been needed only temporarily, to do jobs that most agreed were, in peacetime, men's by right. Men returned to take up their traditional pre-war roles as the breadwinners and women resumed their conventional roles in the home, caring for the children, cleaning and cooking.

Demobilisation started long before the end of hostilities. The ATS began in the middle of July 1944, just six weeks after D-Day. Auxiliary forces, like their male counterparts, were given demob leave and civilian clothes to replace their uniforms. There was no direct equivalent of the servicemen's 'demob suit'. Instead, departing women were given fifty-six clothing coupons and an allowance of £12 10s (£12.50), which was, of necessity, soon increased to £13 16s (£13.80). This was to cover the costs of a hat, 'costume' (usually a dress), scarf, blouse or jumper, stockings, shoes, raincoat and an allowance for alterations – and was as minimal as it sounds. In peacetime austerity Britain, shortages and rationing actually increased as Britain struggled to pay off its war debt. Service men and women returned home to find that their old civilian clothes no longer fitted. Many more discovered that in the drive to 'Make Do and Mend', everything in their civilian wardrobe had long since been recycled and converted into clothes for other members of the family.

Married women were sent home first, and departed initially at such a rate that gaps soon appeared, as the transfer of servicemen to take their places failed to keep pace. Across all the auxiliary services there were still too many jobs for too many women to do, for total demobilisation. The shortages that had made women a necessary part of the forces' manpower were still there. This time, however, the need was for military personnel to deal with the organisation of a return to peacetime society and to help, especially, with the social and physical reconstruction of a devastated Europe.

WAAFs on parade for a royal inspection – the king and queen visiting Tempsford, Bedfordshire, on VE day, May 1945. (Connie Annis/Jonathan Falconer Collection)

So large numbers were sent overseas to help with this enormous postwar task. As a result, many of the auxiliary forces were in service long after the war. Peacetime shortages had an impact everywhere but for the British forces overseas, these often presented as many opportunities as they did limitations.

Nancy Furlong was in the WAAFs in Germany in 1946–7.

I was posted in May 1947 to HQ 84 Group at Celle, Niedersachsen, and in June of that year a friend and I visited Paris. In order to have some civilian clothes to wear I wrote home to my mother asking her to find enough material to make a skirt and jacket. The parcel duly arrived and I took it to a German dressmaker/tailoress in the nearby town. When we opened the material out we found it had a number of moth holes in it! However, the lady did a marvellous job, and combined with a couple of blouses and a pair of white sandals, I was equipped for my visit. I had no German currency so payment was made with packets of real coffee. Most transactions in Germany at that time were paid for with coffee or cigarettes.

Anne Valery recalls that on her trips overseas, she was able to take advantage of the abundance of unrationed coffee in Britain. In Europe, by contrast,

it disappeared after the Nazi occupation. It was still unobtainable after the war. . . . Early in '47, I hitched to Paris with four tins which I sold outside Montparnasse Station, bartering one of the tins for a plait of natural blonde hair. This came from Germany, where blonde plaits had been part of the image of Aryan womanhood. By '47, Germany was so devastated that hair was all that many women had to sell. But few felt guilty about buying it when the papers were still full of gruesome details of the hair cut from victims in the concentration camps. Later I sold the plait to a hairdresser in London and lived on the proceeds until I started work at the BBC.

But in the last days of the war, there were also many important jobs to do at home in Britain, even if the sense of urgency and commitment declined markedly. Betty Sharp recalls the prevailing mood at RAF Duxford:

There was a great deal of talk about demobilisation. Everyone was sorted into a group according to their age and length of service. It was a tremendous task for the Air Ministry to organise. And inevitably there was bound to be a certain amount of dissatisfaction. Some people got priority and were demobbed before their group mainly because they had a job which needed them as soon as possible. I must say that a lot of the fun had gone out of the work and the Other Ranks were beginning to get 'Demob Happy'. A lot of aircrew were redundant but had to be found employment until their demobilisation. And so they were put into administrative jobs. A flight lieutenant was posted in to do mine and I felt very sore about this. But that was the way the way things went.

I made friends with a WAAF catering officer and she and I were in the same group for demobilisation and so we were both waiting for our number to 'come up'. Eventually it did and as we both had the same date for the termination of our service, we decided to spend our demob leave together.

Before we left RAF Chilbolton, we gave a 'Demob Party', which was the recognised thing to do. As the Officers' Mess was not up to much, we asked all and sundry to the local pub. We thought in our innocence that a couple of drinks all round would be the order of the day. But people just stayed around and as the arrangement had been that all drinks were to be on us that evening, funds were running out and it became rather an embarrassment. But we got over it by passing my WAAF cap around for contributions and that saw us through until closing time. Then we all drifted back to the mess and continued there for a very long time. Next day we left with very mixed feelings. We had longed for the day when we should return to 'Civvy Street' and yet we knew that we should miss the service life in so many ways. It had been an extraordinary experience.

My friend and I spent our demob leave walking in the Lake District, staying at Youth Hostels and we had great fun working out our holiday plans. Some of our friends thought we were mad going on a holiday of that sort after the service life; many of them chose to spend a few days in one of the exotic hotels in London, doing the theatres. But it was a great success and by walking well off the beaten track, going from one hostel to another, we saw the Lake District in all its glory.

In 1945, Wren Moira Shepherd was one of the first to be recalled by her peacetime employers. She had been posted from Dover Castle to a submarine base in Dundee. 'The GPO requested my return. I burst into tears as I saw my

The Duchess of Kent inspects WRNS at Dover Command, August 1944. Moira Shepherd, Group Seven's marker, representing HMS Haig *at Rye, remembers 'We were drilled by the Royal Marines at Ramsgate for a national competition and came seventh.'* (M. Shepherd)

own demob instructions coming through on the teleprinter. I returned to Perth to be quickly promoted to a supervisory position before leaving.'

Gwyneth Verdon-Roe stayed in the WRNS until 1946. In late 1945, she wrote to her mother from her quarters in the Rochester Holding Depot in Kent:

We are still here – by the world forgotten. Rumours fly around daily but we are no nearer to hearing our fate. Surplus plotters have become a sad problem. The most reliable news is that we are to have a Selection Board and be remustered but as the only categories with vacancies are for cooks, stewards and clerks the future doesn't look very bright. I only want to be a plotter – or failing that MT [motorised transport].

Eventually, Gwyneth was sent to London to train as a driver:

I can hardly believe I am doing this, it's great. I sat in the back of a lorry watching carefully, then it was my turn in the driver's seat. It is really me trying to drive a 3 ton, 32 horse power lorry on the North Circular Rd, out of London. Our bus driver instructor, called Len, is the nicest, kindest, most patient man imaginable. He says that girls learn to drive more quickly than the men. I feel as proud as Punch sitting in this enormous great lorry, Len beside me looking nervous. I am too small so I have piles of cushions under me and behind me and a large brick under the pedals so my foot can reach them. The steering is heavy as the wheels are so big and the double de-clutch gears make a horrible noise if you don't treat them right. . . . Today I drove 20 miles through traffic and lights and awkward turnings, with convoys on the road, through Hendon, Finchley and Wembley. The afternoon was spent in the classroom learning about Safety First and tomorrow we start on the mechanical dirty work, lying on our backs under the car getting gloriously oily. Our bus man is a darling. He has a son who is a sergeant major, his house has been bombed three times and his wife has all his trainees to tea. He has never taught Wrens before and judging by the remarks from drivers on the road, they haven't seen them before either.

Gwyneth passed her driver's tests and was sent to Greenock, Scotland, part of a group relieving Canadian Wrens who were returning home. She wrote:

I am driving the commander this week in a big car that chuffs like a steam engine. I pick the old boy up at Greenock station, drop him at work and pick

" It's popularly known as ' housemaid's knee,' madam ! Numbers of husbands suffer from it these days."

Cartoon by Gilbert Wilkinson.
(*News Chronicle*)

up his messenger to do the rounds. Then I drink tea until lunchtime when I take the old boy to the harbour. He boozes aboard and sometimes asks me to lunch. At 4.30 p.m. I drive a happy commander, full of gin, to the station. It's a really cushy job.

Gwyneth's demob came just in time for her twenty-first birthday party:

It is worth driving for Naval Stores. The men have been most enthusiastic about finding ingredients for my birthday cake. I would like to send them a slice. I can't imagine being a civilian and I wonder what I will be doing in the future. . . . Suddenly it is all happening so quickly it is hard to take in that the war is over, the three years in the WRNS are nearly over and FREEDOM awaits us. I am sure in years to come I shall have forgotten the miseries of the war and the fleas and will remember only the good times and the friendships.

In the auxiliary forces and in civilian settings, girls (many were only just seventeen) and women surprised themselves with their capacity to suffer hardships, learn new skills and operate under fire. Pre-war women, though not exactly viewed as pathetic, were regarded in the prevailing attitude of the period as being suited only to looking after the home and raising children. Their presence in all-male service environments caused as much comment as might the arrival of an alien from Mars. In 1937, Lieutenant-Commander Kenneth Edwards, RN, wrote in the magazine *Men Only* of the problem of women on board ship – at that time, possible still only as civilian visitors:

> So soon as there is the merest suggestion that the ship should give a dance, opposition of the fiercest kind springs up. Let it be said that this opposition is not due to churlishness or to lack of appreciation of hospitality received. It is due simply to the voice of experience which yells that so soon as women are given the run of the ship at a dance, nothing will be sacred and the most private appurtenance's of one's cabin will become legitimate subjects for conversation and badinage.
>
> Instead of a few intelligent questions, they fire an endless stream of queries, most of which could be easily answered by their own common sense.

The article continued in this vein for a few hundred words. This was a typical, not an extreme, pre-war view. Women were dangerous to have around in a crisis. The concern was often expressed that in such circumstances, women might become hysterical and make a nuisance of themselves by getting in the way of those with real work to do. But by the end of the war, women and girls had demonstrated time and again that they

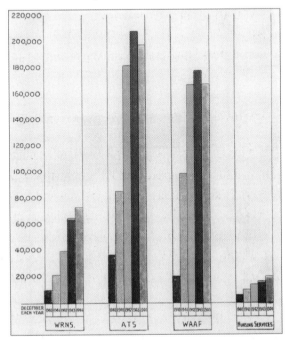

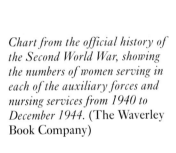

Chart from the official history of the Second World War, showing the numbers of women serving in each of the auxiliary forces and nursing services from 1940 to December 1944. (The Waverley Book Company)

could do any job they were asked to do.

From the onset of women working in their wartime roles, a more typical service view was that of General Sir Frederick Pile. Looking back in 1949 on his experience and observation of women in anti-aircraft batteries, he said, 'I wonder why we were ever such fools as to doubt that the thing would work. . . . The girls lived like men, fought their lights like men and, alas, some of them died like men. Unarmed, they often showed great personal bravery. They earned decorations and they deserved more.'

In the immediate aftermath, there was at least some practical recognition of the contribution to the war effort of women in the auxiliary forces. This came in 1946, when plans were presented to parliament to retain the women's forces permanently. It took three more years before these plans came to fruition, but in 1949 the WRNS were re-formed, the Women's Royal Army Corps, equivalent to the wartime ATS, was created, and the wartime WAAF became the Women's Royal Air Force.

The same rules applied – those serving were non-combatants and on lower pay than their male counterparts. But through attrition and by proving their worth, just as they had in wartime, women in the forces gradually achieved parity. By the end of the twentieth century, with some nudging from European law, women in the armed forces began to compete alongside men for promotion, sharing the same ranks and roles – as they had proved they could do on gun-sites, naval bases, airfields and anywhere else they were sent during the Second World War.

CHAPTER 8

Postscript

Few people today realise the extent of the involvement of women in civilian and military roles in the Second World War. As the war drew to an end, the attention was understandably on – in the popular phrase of the time – 'winning the peace'. Family life, housing, massive reforms in education, health and welfare, and, overseas, the move from Empire to Commonwealth were among the main British concerns in the immediate postwar era.

But as time has passed, this lack of recognition has become more difficult either to justify or to comprehend. Many interviewed for this book spoke of the need for a memorial to the contribution of all women in the last war. The Second World War was, uniquely for this country, a war in which the traditional military approach was only a part of the battle. It was, in Angus Calder's phrase, 'A People's War' in the sense that the contribution of everyone – children and adults, male and female, military and civilian – was vital to the eventual victory.

Without the auxiliary forces, we could not, for example, have run Britain's anti-aircraft defences, its airfields and its naval bases. We could not have kept open lines of communication, and given the fighting forces the essential support and supplies they needed, at home and overseas. Before the war, many women who were later to become members of the auxiliary forces had no idea of, and often no interest in, service life. They performed beyond everyone's expectations, including their own.

Given the general lack of knowledge today about the part women played, a public memorial would be a fitting tribute. It would tell the casual observer that in the last war, ordinary women and girls, who might themselves have been casual observers of world events, did their bit and in doing so made history.

Bibliography

Anon., *Man Power*, HMSO, 1939

Anon., *National Service*, HMSO, 1939

Anon., *Roof Over Britain, the Official History Story of Britain's AA Defences 1939–42*, HMSO, 1942

Bacon, Reginald (ed.)., *Britain's Glorious Navy*, Odhams, 1942

Bigland, Eileen, *The Story of the W.R.N.S.*, Nicholson and Watson, 1946

Boorman, H.R.P., *Hell's Corner 1940*, *Kent Messenger*, 1942

Brayley, Martin and Ingram, Richard, *WWII British Women's Uniforms*, Windrow and Green, 1995

British People at War, Odhams, 1943

Calder, Angus, *The Myth of the Blitz*, Pimlico, 1991

Clayton, Aileen, *The Enemy is Listening*, Hutchinson, 1980

Ewing, Elizabeth, *Women in Uniform Through the Centuries*, Batsford, 1975

Hammerton, Sir John, *The Second Great War*, Amalgamated Press, 1939–46

Hare-Scott, Kenneth, *For Gallantry*, Peter Garnett, 1951

Hough, Richard and Richards, Denis, *The Battle of Britain*, Penguin, 2001

Laughton Mathews, Vera, *Blue Tapestry*, Hollis and Carter, 1949

Mack, Angela, *Dancing on the Waves*, Benchmark Press, 2000

Michie, Allan A. and Graebner, Walter, *Lights of Freedom*, George Allen & Unwin Ltd, 1941

Miller, Lee, *Wrens in Camera*, Hollis and Carter, 1945

Pile, General Sir Frederick, *Ack-Ack*, George G. Harrap and Co., 1949

Sheridan, Dorothy, *Wartime Women – a Mass Observation Anthology*, Phoenix Press, 1990

Smithies, Edward, *Aces, Erks and Backroom Boys*, Cassell, 1990

Starns, Penny, *Nurses at War*, Sutton Publishing, 2000

Terry, Roy, *Women in Khaki*, Columbus Books, 1988

Valery, Anne, *Talking About the War 1939–45: a Personal View*, Michael Joseph, 1991

Ward, Irene, *F.A.N.Y.*, *Invicta*, Hutchinson, 1955

Wilton, Eric, *Centre Crew – A Memory of the Royal Observer Corps*, published privately for members of the Royal Obsever Corps at Bromley, Kent, 1946

Various newspapers and magazines from the 1930s to the 1940s, too numerous to mention individually.

Acknowledgements

I am very grateful to all those who have helped me with this project, especially the following people:

Tom and Anne Allibone
Mary Bateman
Anne Blacoe
Doreen Bradley (née Thompson)
Irene Burchill
Pam Chiles (née Wade)
J. Crickmore
Wyn Crosland
Marion Dare (née Jones)
Joyce Dole
Barbara Emm
Pat Evans
Jonathan Falconer
Nancy Furlong (née Fisher)
Olive Gibbings
Sheila Hamnett
Sheila Holley (née Fenn)
Ivy Hopes
Lorna Kellet
Doris Legg (née Batley)

Susan Lustig
Mary Middleton
Trudy Murray
Hilda Pearce
Ramesh Rajadurai
Mano Ramesh
Joan Ramsay
Betty Sharp
Moira Shepherd
Pamela Smailes
Joyce Stott (née Baister)
Evelyn Sutton
Rob Tagg
Doreen Thompson
Veronica Tournay (née Nary)
Gwyneth Verdon-Roe (née Rogers)
Peggy Wiggett
Carol Williams
Kitty Winfield

Special mention and thanks also to Mike Brown, William Harris-Brown and Ralph Harris-Brown.

Index

Index